POP CULTURE PANICS

Moral panics reveal much about a society's social structure and the sociology embedded in everyday life. This short text examines extreme reactions to American popular culture over the past century, including crusades against comic books, music, and pinball machines, to help convey the "sociological imagination" to undergraduates. Sternheimer creates a critical lens through which to view current and future attempts of modern-day moral crusaders, who try to convince us that simple solutions—like regulating popular culture—are the answer to complex social problems. *Pop Culture Panics* is ideal for use in undergraduate social problems, social deviance, and popular culture courses.

Karen Sternheimer is a sociologist at the University of Southern California, where she is a distinguished fellow at the USC Center for Excellence in Teaching. She is also the author of *Connecting Popular Culture and Social Problems: Why Media is Not the Answer* (2013), *Celebrity Culture and the American Dream: Stardom and Social Mobility* (2011), *Kids These Days: Facts and Fictions About Today's Youth* (2006), *It's Not the Media: The Truth About Pop Culture's Influence on Children* (2003), and is the editor and lead writer for everydaysociologyblog.com. She has provided commentary for NPR, CNN, MSNBC, the History Channel, and Fox News.

D1715201

POP CULTURE PANICS

How Moral Crusaders Construct Meanings of Deviance and Delinquency

Karen Sternheimer

Routledge
Taylor & Francis Group

NEW YORK AND LONDON

9/16/15
LN
$ 39.95

First published 2015
by Routledge
711 Third Avenue, New York, NY 10017

and by Routledge
2 Park Square, Milton Park, Abingdon, Oxon, OX14 4RN

Routledge is an imprint of the Taylor & Francis Group, an informa business

Library of Congress Cataloging-in-Publication Data
Sternheimer, Karen.
    Pop culture panics : how moral crusaders construct meanings of deviance and delinquency / by Karen Sternheimer.
        pages cm
    Includes bibliographical references and index.
    1. Moral panics—United States—History.   2. Popular culture—United States.   3. United States—Moral conditions.   I. Title.
    HN90.M6S74 2015
    302'.17—dc23
    2014024680

ISBN: 978-0-415-74805-6 (hbk)
ISBN: 978-0-415-74806-3 (pbk)
ISBN: 978-1-315-79670-3 (ebk)

Typeset in Adobe Caslon
by ApexCovantage, LLC

Printed and bound in the United States of America by Publishers Graphics, LLC on sustainably sourced paper.

Contents

PREFACE   VII

ACKNOWLEDGMENTS   XI

CHAPTER 1   POP CULTURE CRUSADERS: CONSTRUCTING
            MEANINGS OF DEVIANCE AND DELINQUENCY   1

*Fears that video games would cause violence in the
1990s provide a framework in understanding moral
panics, moral crusades, for how people actively use fears
of popular culture to create new meanings of deviance
and delinquency.*

CHAPTER 2   ANTI-MOVIE CRUSADES: FEARS OF IMMIGRATION,
            URBANIZATION, AND SHIFTS IN CHILDHOOD   23

*The popularity of the movies in the early twentieth
century led to moral crusades to regulate content.
Immigration, urbanization, and shifting experiences
of childhood caused the crusades.*

CHAPTER 3   ANTI-PINBALL CRUSADES: FEARS OF GAMBLING
            AND FREE TIME   49

*Concerns about gambling and organized crime were
projected onto young people during the Great Depression
and World War II. Moral crusades against pinball
highlight anxieties about working-class spaces and about
leisure overtaking the value of hard work.*

CHAPTER 4   ANTI-COMIC BOOK CRUSADES: FEAR OF YOUTH VIOLENCE   73

Postwar fears of delinquency and youth violence reach a fever pitch, which moral crusaders blamed on graphic comic books.

CHAPTER 5   ANTI-MUSIC CRUSADES: FEARS OF RACIAL INTEGRATION, RELIGIOUS PARTICIPATION, AND FREEDOM OF EXPRESSION   105

Much of American popular music derives from African Americans. The widespread success of genres such as jazz, rock and roll, and rap created fears of racial integration. As musicians became revered, religious leaders feared that they would lead young people away from traditional religion.

CHAPTER 6   CONCLUSION: CONTEMPORARY POP CULTURE CRUSADES   133

The growth of social media not only produces fear about a new form of communication, but has created new ways to mount moral crusades.

SELECTED BIBLIOGRAPHY   151

INDEX   155

PREFACE

Can you imagine a place where police censor movies, where books are banned and burned, and authorities outlaw pinball machines?

All of these happened in the United States during the twentieth century. But why?

Pop Culture Panics examines these and other extreme reactions to popular culture over the past century. Rather than simply reactions to troubling content, crusades against video games, movies, pinball machines, comic books, music, and new media are rooted in struggles for power over a group feared as a threat to the status quo.

Campaigns against popular culture remind us that people actively work to construct meanings of deviance, as moral crusaders strive to convince others to see the world as they do, and try to encourage us to further restrict the content of popular culture to protect "us" from "them." Anti-pop culture crusades happen when a group is considered both potentially vulnerable to the influence of media and threatening at the same time. Crusaders successfully used anxieties about social change and the increased leisure time of children and teens to create fear and expand the definition of delinquency.

Using examples from recent history offers readers a critical distance from the emotion of moral crusades. The purpose of this book is to create a critical lens through which to view current and future attempts of modern-day moral crusaders, who try to convince us that simple solutions—like regulating popular culture—are the answer to complex social problems.

Learning From *Pop Culture Panics*

Pop Culture Panics focuses specifically on moral crusaders to better understand what motivated them to wage campaigns against popular culture. In most cases, moral crusaders feel threatened by social changes they connect with a new form of popular culture.

The context and timing are crucial for understanding why people launched crusades against silent movies, pinball machines, comic books, jazz, rock and roll, rap, and video games. *Pop Culture Panics* explores how fears of immigration, urbanization, anti-Semitism and the reduction of child labor sparked concerns about movies almost as soon as they became popular in the first decade of the twentieth century.

Pinball machines may now seem innocuous—and sources of nostalgia—but when they first appeared in the 1930s they coincided with the rise in organized crime and concerns that young people would gamble rather than work.

Comic books aroused postwar anxieties about the new experiences of childhood. Mostly out of the paid labor force with more leisure time and discretionary spending money than ever before, the new favored pastime of "idle" children awakened fears that juvenile delinquency would skyrocket, with their graphic crime stories and macabre themes.

As postwar children became teens, many began listening to a new genre, rock and roll, a hybrid of many musical traditions largely created by African American musicians. Coinciding with the civil rights movement and challenges to Jim Crow laws, crusades about early rock and roll were rooted in concerns about racial integration. As music became an integral part of baby boomers' experiences of adolescence, some religious leaders feared that rock was displacing the role of traditional religion in young people's lives, and that the music itself was a satanic force. Moral crusaders claimed that hidden satanic messages could be heard on some records when played backwards, and called for legislation to create labels and warn parents of the alleged threat.

Throughout the twentieth century and into the twenty-first, entertainment choices have expanded dramatically and become more segmented. From seeing movies and playing pinball in public places to reading comic books and listening to music in private, controlling access to popular culture has become increasingly difficult, drawing concerns that adults can no longer limit what their children see, hear, and know. Today, smartphone technology makes it even more difficult to control, creating concerns about "sexting," reflecting fears that without restraint many young people will engage in this risky behavior (although adults are more likely to do so than teens).

This same technology creates opportunities for new moral crusades. Not only about new technologies such as social networking, but moral crusaders can use social media to spread concerns about others without traditional media gatekeepers. Micro crusades can take place through new media, as groups that view the *Harry Potter* series as satanic can communicate with one another and organize outside of traditional large-scale media platforms.

Ultimately, *Pop Culture Panics* explores how meanings of deviance are socially constructed, created by people who seek to persuade others that controlling the content of popular culture will stave off the "threat" of the feared group, be they immigrants, people of color, or teens. Behind the crusades against popular culture are groups that struggle to hold onto a past that they see as slipping away, as demographic and economic shifts create changes that lead to fears about and for young people.

ACKNOWLEDGMENTS

I am very grateful for the opportunity to publish this book with Routledge. Thanks to Steve Rutter and Margaret Moore, editor and editorial assistant, for your enthusiasm and support for this project. Margaret worked particularly hard to secure permission for the images included in the text. The insightful comments of Clinton Sanders (University of Connecticut) and Dustin Kidd (Temple University) were most helpful and I appreciate the time they took to review the manuscript.

Continued thanks go to my colleagues in the sociology department at the University of Southern California, who have continued to nurture my intellectual curiosity and continue to champion my accomplishments. I am particularly grateful for the long-term support of Tim Biblarz, Lynne Casper, Elaine Bell Kaplan, Mike Messner, Molly Ranney, Sally Raskoff, and Rhacel Salazar Parreñas. I am also grateful for the continued support of Karl Bakeman and Eileen Connell.

I have had the pleasure of working with many great students at USC who inspire me to learn more about the subjects I teach in order to share more with them. Several students directly provided research assistance for this book, including researching historical newspapers, magazines, and books for this project. Thanks to Presley Bard, Juliette Cooke, Brandon Estrada, Stacy Han, and Koree Yancy for their enthusiasm and assistance.

Thanks to my extended family for your continued support and understanding when work on this and previous projects may cut into visiting time. I appreciate the excitement about my work that my aunts and uncles, Barbara Cohen, Saul and Ellen Fettner, and Larry and Nancy Friedman, have shown for many years. I am very grateful for the support of my parents, Lee and Toby, my siblings and their significant others, Laura and Rich, Linda and Jacob, and nephews Eli and Julian. And thanks to Mike, for helping with the images, and for monopolizing my leisure time.

1

POP CULTURE CRUSADERS

Constructing Meanings of Deviance
and Delinquency

Around lunchtime on April 20, 1999, two students at a Colorado high school carried out a planned attack. Heavily armed, they opened fire on classmates in the school's cafeteria and library. Breaking news coverage broadcast the frenzied scene to the nation and the world. Sobbing students ran from the school, as others were carried out on gurneys, bloodied from the events inside. How many students were injured? Were there more suspects at large? When would the violence end—at Columbine High School that day and around the country more generally?

On that day, two students killed twelve of their classmates and a teacher before killing themselves.

Frightened parents throughout the country wondered whether their children were safe at school, and wanted reassurance that this couldn't happen to their children. Politicians promised that they would do something. Commentators looked for sources of blame for the seemingly unexplainable: how could two boys from an affluent neighborhood, attending what appeared to be an excellent school, do something so evil?

Popular culture, particularly first-person shooter video games, quickly became a central explanation for the event. In a Gallup Poll conducted the next day, 49 percent of respondents thought violent media contributed to the problem, and 52 percent thought "stricter regulation" of media content was the answer.[1] "Violent Video Was Just a Dress Rehearsal," said a *New York Post* headline, noting that the two gunmen were "obsessed with violent video games."[2] An article on the front page of the *New York Times* the same day noted the specific games that the shooters enjoyed.[3] For many observers troubled by the content of violent games, it seemed reasonable that video games could have played a role. After all, the graphics within the games had become far more realistic than when video game technology first became popular in the 1970s, and sales had more than doubled between 1995 and 2000, according to one estimate.[4] The violent games encouraged players to shoot and kill characters; would this teach young kids that it is okay, even pleasurable to shoot others?

Media coverage zeroed in on the video game explanation; magazines, newspapers, and cable news repeatedly mentioned video games in stories about the shootings.[5] With millions of young gamers, some wondered whether school shootings could become as common as a schoolyard brawl, which seemed a nostalgic throwback to simpler times. Were 1990s teens completely out of control, so awash in violent media that they had no sense of right and wrong? What could be done to stop teens before they kill again?

Talk of Congressional hearings and further regulation followed; something must be done, proponents argued, to prevent the next Columbine. In response, grieving family members filed lawsuits against video game makers, schools installed high-tech security systems, and "zero tolerance" policies were put in place around the country. Problem solved?

Despite emotional claims that video games were causing teens to kill their peers nationwide, youth violence rates had actually *dropped* during the 1990s; school shootings had declined as well.[6] There was no new wave of killing among youth in the 1990s or in the 2000s, as youth violence rates continued to decline and have remained flat. Video games were not causing a violence epidemic, because the tragic incident that took place at Columbine High School that day in 1999 was an anomaly, not the new normal.

Complaints about video games are part of a long history of suspicion about how young people spend their leisure time. As we will see throughout this book, in the past people had similar concerns about movies, comic books, pinball machines, and music—so much so that at one point police censored movies, cities banned pinball machines, Congress pondered regulating comic books, and groups burned books and records. All have been blamed for somehow damaging children's and teens' moral compass, as critics continually worry about the next generation based on their pastime of choice.

This book explores how and why activists have waged campaigns against popular culture throughout recent American history, and how this process shapes the way we think about both deviance and juvenile delinquency. This chapter uses fears of video games and youth violence as a contemporary example in order to address the central questions of this book:

- Why has popular culture historically been a site of struggle and concern?
- What are moral panics, how are they created, and why do they happen?
- What are moral crusaders and moral entrepreneurs? What do they stand to gain from crusades against popular culture?
- What are folk devils? How and why do moral crusaders create them? How does the creation of folk devils shape meanings of deviance?
- What is the importance of timing and context in anti-popular culture crusades? How is the timing of these crusades related to growing concerns about juvenile delinquency?

In several of my previous books, I explored the disproportional fears of both media and youth. In this book, I focus on the campaigns against media more generally, looking closely at who leads them and why. The answers go well beyond the content of popular culture itself.

Concerns About Popular Culture

The term "popular culture" is used so regularly it is often taken for granted. Is popular culture different from other forms of culture? The problem in defining popular culture is that it is rooted in what people *think* about the culture being categorized as popular, and it has no clear singular definition.[7] Yet popular culture has historically been seen as problematic, partly for its content and partly in defining its audience. A discussion of competing theories of popular culture is far beyond the scope of this book; what follows is a very brief overview.

Within sociology, there has been a long-running debate between the notions of "high culture" and what has at times been called "mass culture." High culture has traditionally been defined as the bastion of the elites and connotes the high status of its participants. Today, we might view classical music, opera, ballet, and some forms of theater and art as forms of culture regarded as having high artistic merit, and predominantly enjoyed by those with wealth, status, and power rather than "the masses."

In contrast, mass culture, more often today called popular culture, would include forms of entertainment that are created for a large audience, primarily for profit, and enjoyed by a wider, perhaps less discriminating audience. While "high culture" might be considered enriching, educational, and aesthetically important, popular culture has been dismissed as unimportant, vulgar, and even dangerous, especially since some have feared that "mass" audiences are not savvy consumers of culture and will thoughtlessly adopt the messages in the forms of popular culture they consume.[8] Sociologist Paul Lopes describes how critics of popular culture often create "cultural hierarchies" to condemn and attempt to restrict content they see as troublesome.[9] Many of the arguments about the dangers of popular culture claim it is harmful to young people, and should be censored, eliminated, or sanitized to protect children.

However, the distinction between the two is problematic: high culture can become popular culture and vice versa. The so-called elites might enjoy forms of popular culture and non-elite people might like forms of "high culture." The two might merge and thus become indistinguishable. And as scholars in sociology and other disciplines such as cultural studies have observed, popular culture is not simply meaningless drivel, but is a central part of how groups and individuals construct meanings of their social worlds.

Sociologist Herbert Gans challenges the usefulness of these categories, and refutes long-held belief that popular culture is a danger to the broader culture and a threat to those who enjoy it. He challenges the notion that the public is somehow victimized by popular culture, and argues "against the idea that only the cultural expert knows what is good for people and for society." Gans also discusses that culture can create conflict. "In heterogeneous societies, the struggles between diverse groups and aggregates over the allocation of resources and power are not limited to strictly economic and political issues, but also extend to cultural ones."[10]

We see these struggles play out in concerns about video games and other forms of popular culture. Rather than just about the content of video games—which is certainly worth criticizing sometimes—the struggles over popular culture have more to do with *who* its participants are, their social status, as well as the status and power of their critics. Video game players are presumed to be young, thought to be easily manipulated by the games' content, prone to violence, and considered a threat for this reason.

Bolstered by a number of Supreme Court decisions supporting First Amendment rights, as well as market conditions increasing competition for consumers, the subject matter of popular culture expanded during the twentieth century. Bans and restrictions of media content relaxed, upholding freedom of expression and offering much for moral crusaders to campaign against, as movies, music, books, games, and other media no longer had to conform to narrow standards of respectability. Over the course of the century, content became less sanitized, and popular culture offered increasingly explicit depictions of sexuality, violence, and other controversial topics.

The technological changes of the twentieth century played a role in concerns about popular culture. Since the beginning of the century, media consumption has shifted from the public sphere with movies to being increasingly private and segmented, making it more difficult to monitor and control. With each form of new media came new worries that they would bring harm, that vulnerable populations would learn the wrong values in an ever-enticing media environment. This shift has made content more niche-specific and less targeted to a general audience, leading to distinct "taste communities" often demarcated by age, and perhaps less appealing to adults and others in positions of authority. Critics of video games, particularly those who believed that they could lead to real violence by consumers, were likely a generation or two removed from playing them. The greater distance from a form of popular culture, the easier it is to fear it and its consumers.

What Are Moral Panics?

The 1990s school shootings led to a *moral panic* about video games. A moral panic is a widespread fear that arises which is dramatically out of proportion with the actual threat. The fear is often accompanied by emotional demands that something be done to stop it in order to preserve the basic morals of a society. According to sociologists Erich Goode and Nachman Ben-Yehuda, a moral panic is a: "strong, widespread (although not necessarily universal) fear or concern that evil doings are afoot, that certain enemies of society are trying to harm some or all of the rest of us."[11]

First explored in depth by Cohen in his study of disproportional fears of youth violence in a seaside British resort during 1964, Cohen describes how moral panics are about more than the feared events themselves, but about concerns about a "spreading social disease" that seem to be a "sign of the times."[12] Likewise, concerns about video games took on a sense of urgency and moral outrage: did games makers manufacture a product that portrayed murder in a positive light? Would the games teach its players to kill and eventually harm others, much like a communicable disease?

While a panic is a highly emotional overreaction, a *moral* panic has a component of righteousness, framing the issue as a battle between good and evil. A rampage shooting, where young people are killed en masse at school, is easily seen as an evil, immoral act, and concerns about video games centered around claims that these games harmed the moral judgment of impressionable young people. Moral panics focus on people, groups, or things that seem to threaten the very moral fiber of society.

Moral panics aren't only about popular culture, of course. Panics about communist threats, immigrants, and the Japanese Americans during World War II are all examples of disproportional and widespread fears that emerged in history. Goode and Ben Yehuda describe panics about witchcraft in European history, drug scares in the United States and in Israel, as well as fears of "sexual psychopaths" in the mid-twentieth century.[13] Others have examined moral panics in the US and Britain focusing on child sexual abuse, satanic rituals, welfare abusers, random violence, gangs, pornography, HIV/AIDS, ecstasy, and raves.[14]

These examples highlight that moral panics aren't necessarily completely made-up issues; to call something a moral panic is not to deny that something exists. While no evidence supports the fear that Japanese Americans were plotting against the US government during World War II, gang violence does exist, some children *are* sexually abused, there are people who misuse welfare, and some people are victims of random violence. Concerns about popular culture don't happen in a vacuum. Rates of youth violence *did* rise between the late 1980s and early 1990s, leading activists and politicians to look for possible causes and sources of control in order to reduce future threats. Video games *did* become more popular in the 1990s, with graphics becoming more realistic and more ubiquitous with the advent of online gaming.

But moral panics around these issues exaggerate the frequency and manner of the problem. For instance, Mary de Young writes about panics surrounding daycare centers in the US in the 1980s, where hundreds of children were allegedly sexually abused. The snowball effect of media coverage placed more and more daycare centers under suspicion, despite the fact that most of the claims of abuse went unproven.[15] Likewise, Joel Best debunked the notion that in the 1990s drivers were suddenly committing "road rage" against strangers in large numbers, often for no reason, despite scary news reports suggesting this was indeed a new trend.[16] Craig Reinarman examines how the timing of drug scares is perhaps more important than the effects of the drugs themselves, as is the feared group that becomes the target of restrictive laws.[17] Moral panics can make an issue seem new, growing worse, and an imminent threat even if it is not any of these things in actuality.

What Are Moral Crusaders and Moral Entrepreneurs?

Moral panics typically require people to convince others that a problem exists and something must be done about it; some people are more successful than others in convincing the public that a serious moral threat exists. Even if the public outrage explodes spontaneously, someone is usually there to fan the flames and take on an activist role as a *moral crusader*.

A moral crusader tries to get the public's attention for a cause that they see as creating a threat to the overall wellbeing of society. They often appear in the news media trying to convince others that, unless something is done, more people will be hurt by what they cast as a new and growing problem. Moral crusaders see themselves as battling against evil and often use highly emotional arguments to win people over to their cause. They also often offer what they consider to be a solution to the problem. Within the anti-video game crusade, multiple groups, activists, and politicians took up the cause, promoting further restriction of content in order to protect against the threat they believed the games posed.

Moral crusades highlight competing values. In the case of video games, the competing values are between freedom of expression and control, who should be controlled, and who should do the controlling. Those arguing for control of video games suggest that it's not just the games, but who has access to them—namely, young people—that are central to the problem. Claims that children will be harmed are great attention-getting devices for moral crusaders. As we will see, historically moral crusades that began against other groups, such as immigrants and/or people of color, often gained the most traction by focusing on young people as both potential victims and villains. Typically in the case of moral crusades against popular culture, calls for enhanced government regulation are made to protect the rest of us from their alleged threat. Every high-profile incident of youth violence, especially school shootings with mass casualties, seemed to give more credence to the video game claim, and thus the need for more control and less freedom.

Sociologist Howard Becker describes such activists as *moral entrepreneurs*, people who may also experience a rise in status due to their leadership role. Moral entrepreneurs often work creatively to influence media coverage, getting their cause(s) in the limelight as often as possible. They are often charismatic, or successfully draw in others to their cause to become spokespeople.[18] While there is a great deal of overlap between the concepts of moral crusader and moral entrepreneur, I view moral entrepreneurs as more focused on potential personal gains than moral crusaders.

Being a moral entrepreneur can become a full-time job, and occasionally a well-paid job at that. One national media appearance can lead to dozens of other media appearances, especially if producers think that the claim is a hot new story. Never wanting to be left out of trending news items, it's not unusual for producers to see a story on a competing network or radio show and want to cover the same story themselves. All of this coverage can lead to donations to an advocacy group (which can be comprised of one claims-maker with a knack for writing press releases), freeing up their time to do more media appearances.

Moral crusaders typically feel passionately that their cause is one of moral necessity, and although they might experience personal gain by bringing it to light, this is not only about bolstering their ego or bank accounts as much as it is solving what they consider to be a problem. Driven by their cause, they most probably don't make a living from their involvement, and if they do it is likely modest. Instead, being a moral crusader is likely to help brand them as an expert on the issue, which enables them to define the issue as a serious problem, for which something must be done. A moral crusader might have several causes that they promote, and might start off as a public figure before championing their cause.

They serve ready to appear on the news when a major story breaks that seems to justify their cause. A highly-publicized incident of youth violence can become an opportunity to explain why further control is needed. As Cohen observed, "It is clear that people who denounce deviance may at the same time have a vested interest in seeing deviance perpetuated, at least temporarily, until the phenomenon loses its 'sales value.'"[19]

Moral crusaders against video games include a former journalist who founded an advocacy group (although it's unclear if there is anyone in the group besides the founder), which advocates against all toys that involve violence, putting out a list around holiday shopping season of the top ten toys to avoid buying for children. Working separately, a former Marine sergeant wrote a book claiming that video games were used by the military as "murder simulators," suggesting that if the military uses video games to get soldiers to kill, they must make children kill as well (the Marines challenged his claim following his book's release).

Both of these moral crusaders have received prime-time news coverage and testified during Senate hearings on video games and violence. For claims-makers, getting the attention of political leaders is a central goal: not only is there built-in attention to an issue when it becomes part of a political agenda, but new laws can be proposed—often the ultimate purpose of moral crusades.

Politicians regularly ride the wave of moral crusades, in some cases acting as moral entrepreneurs themselves. Aligning with a cause that seems to take the moral high ground poses little political risk. President Bill Clinton spoke out against video games after the Columbine shootings, offering him a chance to perhaps reclaim some moral authority following a highly publicized sex scandal. Particularly after the public sentiment seemed to turn against video games, senators who challenged video game manufacturers at public hearings could demonstrate to their constituents that they were working to protect their children. They can also avoid the political landmine of challenging the National Rifle Association's (NRA) position on gun ownership, yet still appear to be taking action.

Despite numerous congressional hearings over the past two decades, little has come from them other than sound-bites and calls for self-restraint by video game manufacturers. In 1994, the video game industry created its own rating system, labeling some games "Mature" and "Adults Only." Beyond self-regulation, the First Amendment prevents government intervention in video game content, bolstered by a US Supreme Court decision in 2011, which determined that states cannot restrict access to games based on age, and that video games were protected free speech.[20] Since no legal changes have been—or for the most part, can be—made, moral crusaders continue to demand that something be done, and their work goes on.

What Are Folk Devils?

Moral crusaders need something—and someone—to crusade against. Without a group who crusaders think needs further punishment or control, they have no crusade.

Cohen's term for those cast as evil-doers is "folk devils": the people, group, or characteristic that becomes portrayed in a uniformly threatening fashion. Cohen explains that "the successful creation of folk devils rests on their stereotypical portrayal as atypical actors against a background that is overtypical."[21]

Moral crusaders defined video game manufacturers, as well as troubled youth who play the games, as morally suspect. Critics charged games makers with peddling games that triggered impressionable youth to take up arms and become violent. In his weekly radio address, President Clinton called out the industry, saying, "I ask you to make every video game and movie as if your own children were watching it."[22] Generalizations about young people's vulnerability to media imagery implied that any young player could be a ticking time bomb. By characterizing video games makers and young people as beyond the boundaries of moral acceptability, moral crusaders could position themselves as on the side of good, and the others on the side of evil.

To properly demonize video games, claims-makers conveniently omit the many other instances when young people are exposed to violence, especially in their everyday lives beyond media. By suggesting that video games include graphic depictions of violence that normalize the experience for players, they imply that without video games players wouldn't have firsthand information about violence.

Moral crusaders cast folk devils as doing serious and lasting damage to society, whether intentionally or not. Video game manufacturers may not be trying to create lasting harm, but claims-makers portray them as greedy profiteers, not taking responsibility for the harm they allegedly cause because they make money from the presumed bloodlust of its consumers.

In his analysis of the Salem witch trials, sociologist Kai Erikson writes of how casting some people as dangerous serves to reinforce the boundaries of a society, and reaffirm a moral center. In effect, defining outsiders helps to reaffirm—or even create—the character of those whose behavior remains within such boundaries. Without defining enemies we might not know who we as a society are; casting some people as folk devils reaffirms that the rest of us share similar values, and thus helps to define who we are as a society.[23] Senate hearings on video games, held in 1993 and 1994, were a powerful way to delineate between "them" and "us": those who hold "our" values, and those who do not. So although no new legislation would restrict video game content, the hearings served a purpose. They attempted to define who poses a danger to the rest of us.

Moral crusaders' creation of folk devils ultimately serves as an attempt to create new meanings of deviance, and is an important reminder that people actively try and convince us that behavior is acceptable or beyond the pale. By studying moral crusades, we get a behind the scenes look at how deviance is socially constructed, how the meanings of deviance are created through by people. Deviance cannot exist until people work to define something as such.

The constructionist perspective unpacks the ways in which we think about deviance, asking more than just "is it wrong?" but "*who* insists that something is wrong?" and "why is something considered wrong in one circumstance, in one time or place, but not another?" The constructionist perspective considers who might benefit from defining an individual, group, or behavior as deviant. Who might benefit from, say, restricting sales of violent video games? Moral crusaders argue that we all would, that people would be safer and children less violent. But the constructionist approach requires that we ask who *does not* benefit from further control: young people who play video games become characterized as dangerous and face increasing scrutiny and perhaps legal intervention. Now, perhaps that sounds fine to many people, based on age or socioeconomic status, if they are unlikely to find themselves restricted further because of this new way of constructing deviance. But for those with perhaps less social power, those who might already be marginalized, this increased control is related to existing hostilities faced from people who already see them as troublemakers. Thus, the work of moral crusaders reinforces the process of constructing people as part of problem populations.

In contrast to a more nuanced understanding of the social construction of deviance, students often learn that deviance is the violation of a norm, but this is a rather limited definition. First, we don't all agree on what constitutes norms or violations. People certainly don't all agree about whether violent video games are "deviant," despite moral crusaders' attempts for the public to agree with them that they are and thus should be condemned.

Battles over what kinds of popular culture are problematic are clear examples of this disagreement, as are disagreements about how to respond to perceived violations. Should content be banned? Restricted for some? Open to all? And why might we be concerned about some content at one time but not another? If deviance is just the violation of a norm, how and why do norms change, and who changes them? The constructionist perspective reminds us that people create meanings of deviance; we do not simply just decide something violates norms collectively without the help of others convincing us that we should see things their way.

The constructionist approach to deviance also examines the importance of power. In this book we will see that, traditionally, those in positions of power have had more opportunities to shape public opinion and effectively work to redefine meanings of deviance. Historically, crusades against popular culture have been waged by those who have status and some form of power. They might be clergy members or elected officials or can otherwise get media coverage. Those in positions of power or influence can also shape the construction of policies and laws. These restrictions do not merely reflect public sentiment—although they might have many supporters. Often dissenters are demonized, characterized as a serious threat to the wellbeing of society, especially to children, and may even experience a decline in social status.

Understanding deviance requires us to be critical when activists and authorities encourage us to view others as threats. Deviance is the end result of the work of those trying to convince others to place restrictions on individuals or groups seen as unraveling the moral fabric of society. Anti-video game crusades sought to restrict who could purchase video games and pressure games makers to avoid violent content. Most troubling, this crusade was based on the false notion that young people had become more violent, opening the door for more punitive school policies that served to criminalize young people in a backdrop where the juvenile justice system was gradually being dismantled in favor of more punishment and less rehabilitation.

Timing, Context, and Concerns About Delinquency

According to Goode and Ben-Yehuda, "moral panics arise in troubled times, during which a serious *threat* is sensed to the interests or values of the society."[24] Panics and crusades happen at particular places and times for a reason, especially when structural and cultural shifts take place. Cohen notes they are more likely to happen when "societies are more open than usual to appeals to . . . consensus," as often takes place if there seems to be a threat that something will change society for the worst, particularly a "moral laxity" feared thanks to a particular change.[25]

Claims-makers don't create folk devils out of thin air. It helps if there is already pre-existing hostility towards the group. In the 1990s, concerns about children as cold-blooded killers made their way into Congress and speeches by President Clinton, who warned that something had to be done to control the coming danger. In 1997, Florida Representative Bill McCollum wrote that "Violent juvenile crime has reached epidemic proportions, and state juvenile-justice systems are incapable of handling this crisis."[26] He called for support of legislation then making its way through Congress that would make penalties for juveniles committing violence more severe. He certainly wasn't alone—criminologists had predicted that a new wave of juvenile criminals was on the horizon, dubbed "super-predators" by John Dilulio in 1995.[27]

This led to legislation that largely dismantled the juvenile justice system, making it easier to try young people as adults in most states and taking away many of the discretionary powers of juvenile court judges.[28] Lawmakers argued that in order to prevent future youth violence, we would need to enact stiffer penalties and "get tough" on juvenile crime, implying that juvenile courts were too lenient and that young criminals knew it. (Two major US Supreme Court decisions have since ruled some of the "get tough" changes unconstitutional; juveniles cannot be sentenced to death nor can laws require mandatory life sentences for juveniles.[29])

Fears about young predators followed a moral panic in the 1980s about so-called "crack babies," children born to crack-addicted mothers who would allegedly be uneducable and prone to lives of crime. These mostly poor children of color living in urban centers would need more police oversight (but somehow not more special education resources). The crack baby threat never materialized, and in fact far more babies are born with fetal alcohol syndrome than exposure to illegal drugs.[30] But the widespread concern about young people remained, making it easier to presume that video games could light a pre-existing fuse, turning this "new breed" of youth into violent Stepford-like killers.

Ironically, juvenile violence rates—and violent crime rates in general—had been declining. Between 1996 and 2005, juvenile arrests fell 25 percent; homicide arrests fell 47 percent, and would continue to fall in the 2000s.[31] The predicted wave of super-predators never arrived, but this didn't mean the fear abated. Likewise, concerns about youth violence rose at various points throughout the twentieth century, independent of actual youth crime trends. As sociologist Joel Best points out, social problems need not be based on statistical reality for issues to be defined as problems by the public and policymakers.[32]

As we will see throughout this book, fears about juvenile delinquency are not necessarily rooted in criminal activity, but on the shifting notion of what it means to be an adolescent. Throughout the twentieth century, young people left the paid labor force and were increasingly considered more like children than young adults. Nonconformity, often expressed through the embrace of popular culture that many adults didn't like, came to be equated with delinquency. Punishment for status offenses, or behaviors that are only illegal for minors—such as curfew violations, truancy, drinking, or even disobedience—expanded during the twentieth century as expectations for adolescents' behavior changed.

Fears about the effects of video games are thus not just about video games, but about the pre-existing concerns about juvenile violence. Coupled with technological changes taking place, video games, and the young people that played them, seemed particularly threatening.

Video games appear to provide a tidy explanation for why young people from suburbia might act out violently while ignoring the important contexts of violence itself. Although not necessarily the intention of moral crusaders, their campaigns typically serve to deflect attention away from other important issues: family violence and instability, bullying, mental health issues, and decreased funding for education, most notably reducing the number of school counselors, as well as increased focus on standardized test scores, leading to cuts in other curricula not part of the testing rubric. For young people on the margins, the get-tough legal climate and reduced opportunities for alternative curricula in school can lead to even greater alienation and criminalization.

Most youth violence takes place in areas plagued by poverty, high unemployment, illegal drug trade, and limited opportunity. Focusing on various forms of media, like video games, helps us ignore the structural conditions of urban centers and why neighborhoods divested of industry, basic amenities like grocery chains, and other necessities breed violence. Focusing on video games makes understanding the roots of violence seem simple, when in fact it is complex and based on decades of economic changes and policy shifts that enable entire communities to decay.

Moral panics tend to mutate, ebb, and flow over time. Fears about the impact of one form of media may transform into a concern about another form of popular culture while using essentially the same arguments. In recent years, fears of video games have subsided somewhat, despite their even wider reach with smartphones and realistic graphics. Like dormant viruses, they can re-emerge at different times, as they did after a 20-year-old massacred 20 children and 6 adults at Sandy Hook Elementary School in Connecticut in 2012.

So why did the video game panic ebb? After the attacks of September 11, 2001, terrorists, not teens, were considered the biggest threat to Americans' safety. Public attention turned to immigrants, initially from the Middle East, and those of Muslim faith, whether American or not, as potential threats. Video games continued to become more mainstream as smartphone apps and consoles such as Nintendo's Wii appealed to a broader audience than just teens. And while many people still may associate video gaming with teens, according to industry data the average gamer in 2013 was 31 years old and had been playing for 14 years.[33] As more and more people have grown up playing—and continue to play—video games in various forms, it has become less of a marginalized activity and harder to associate with "outsiders."

Introduction to Chapters

As we will see in upcoming chapters, the fear that popular culture will lead to troubling behavior among youth is by no means new. This book looks primarily at twentieth-century anti-media crusades. The video game panic follows a long line of similar complaints about movies, pinball, comic books, and music, all to be explored in this book using accounts in news stories compiled through Lexis-Nexis database searches as a main source. Using historical news accounts presents the opportunity to see how anti-popular culture crusades were communicated to a broader audience, albeit through the filter of the reporters and editors. Although limited to the newspapers that participate in the database, the sources used are mostly major newspapers from large cities and provide a rich glimpse of these crusades.

Sometimes it is easier to think critically about moral crusades from the past; we may get so caught up in the emotion of today's moral crusades that critical analysis can be difficult. So while the last chapter will consider contemporary crusades, including using smartphone technology to send sexually explicit messages, or "sexting," as well as campaigns claiming *Harry Potter* books and movies promote the occult, most of this book focuses on fears about popular culture from the past in order to dissect how and why these campaigns happen, and what they teach us about the construction of deviance and juvenile delinquency.

The first historical crusade we will consider is one about movies from their origins at the start of the twentieth century. Anti-movie crusades emerged when concerns about immorality accompanied more leisure time for youth and the working class and a dramatic economic shift in the US. As with video games, movie content was not the only thing that moral crusaders were afraid of. Urbanization, immigration, and the shifting demographics made some native-born, rural, white Protestants concerned about growing changes in American society. Fear that some new arrivals did not share their "American values" drove the moral crusade against movies, especially as they became part of most Americans' weekly entertainment. Some of the early crusades were explicitly anti-immigrant, and notably anti-Semitic. As these groups assimilated into American society, they seemed less foreign and attacks on them became less socially acceptable and mostly faded away.

But as young people gradually left the paid labor force, new notions of childhood innocence emerged. Childhood became equated with purity and concerns about the "corrupting" influence of movies gained traction with moral crusaders and the public. So while beliefs that movies would have negative effects on minority ethnic groups largely fell out of favor, concerns about childhood innocence gained traction and would set the stage for future moral crusades. Warning the public that some evil could come to their children from a new form of popular culture became very effective.

While complaints about movies won't come as a big shock to twenty-first-century readers, you might be surprised to learn that pinball machines and comic books also raised the ire of moral crusaders in the middle of the twentieth century. With postwar prosperity came growing suburbs and the extension of adolescence as a time of leisure—and serious concerns about juvenile delinquency. Just like nickelodeons and movie theaters earlier in the century, arcades came to represent danger, as concerns about idleness grew at a time when fewer and fewer teens worked full-time for wages.

As threatening as arcades may have seemed, the isolation of comic book reading likewise served as a source of concern. With greater leisure time, discretionary income, and the growing recognition of distinct teen and children's markets for popular culture, moral crusaders accused comic books of being instruction manuals for violence. Their colorful graphics a departure from the prior generation of magazines, many comic books did (and still do) include images of fantasy violence. Like with video games, crusaders argued that comic books could be directly linked to specific incidents of youth violence, leading to Senate hearings and—just as with video games—industry self-regulation.

Music has also been the target of moral crusades over the twentieth century, from concerns about the dangers of jazz to the birth of rock and roll through the end of the century with heavy metal and rap. Woven into the fears that these forms of music would create violence, promote promiscuity, satanic worship, and drug use are anxieties about shifting race relations and the secularization of American society. As a backlash of sorts to the decline of segregation and increasing focus on individual liberties during the last half of the century, music symbolizes freedom of expression and served to help reduce racial barriers. Moral crusades against various forms of music serve as a proxy battle for a host of issues, providing cover against accusations of racism.

Moral crusades are inevitable, especially in our hyper-mediated age, where news—often little more than infotainment—is driven by emotion rather than journalistic standards. To compete with other forms of entertainment, our sources of news, be they online, in print, or on television, often focus on the dramatic and unusual, and thus are a great breeding ground for moral panics. Moral crusaders now can write blogs, post a YouTube video, or appear on the countless hours of cable news that producers need to fill with dramatic content. Their reach has probably never been greater than now.

It should also come as no surprise that many contemporary moral crusades center on new technology available in the internet age, where communication is largely open and difficult to control and monitor. Smartphones that enable rapid transmission of text and images reflect the reduced ability to control teen communication, leading to fears about promiscuity and the media-made term "sexting." Adding the technological element to an already-existing issue dramatizes the problem, reflecting anxiety during a time of flux. Contemporary crusades no longer need actual crusaders. News sources often craft stories using techniques borrowed from the emotion-driven style of moral crusades, inviting audiences to use social media to share their opinions. News organizations are not necessarily interested in a particular cause or outcome, like traditional moral crusaders might be. Instead, ratings and earnings trump heartfelt belief in a cause, perhaps a more cynical version of Becker's moral entrepreneurs.

Moral crusades are ultimately about a search for social order in changing times and the ongoing need to create outsiders in order to redefine what it means to be an insider. Crusades are likely to happen when enough people perceive or fear that the so-called outsiders are threatening the moral order of a society—whether they actually pose any danger or not. In the end, regardless of moral crusaders' intentions, their actions reflect an attempt to shore up the social status of dominant groups. While not necessarily effective for controlling popular culture in the long term, moral crusades serve an important purpose in their attempt to draw moral boundaries around a changing society.

Notes

1. Richard Bennedetto, "Blame is Placed on Parents, Media," *USA Today*, April 22, 1999, p. 3A.
2. Maria Alvarez and Tracy Connor, "Violent Video Was Just a Dress Rehearsal," *New York Post*, April 23, 1999, p. 3.
3. Jodi Wilgoren and Dirk Johnson, "Terror in Littleton," *New York Times*, April 23, 1999, p. A1.
4. See "Game Industry Sales Data," *The Acagamic*, www.acagamic.com/research/stats/game-industry-sales-data.

5. See Karen Sternheimer, "Do Video Games Kill?," *Contexts* 6, no. 1 (2007), pp. 13–17.
6. Federal Bureau of Investigation, *Uniform Crime Reports for the United States, 1964–1999* (Washington, DC: US Department of Justice, 2000).
7. For more discussion, see Dominic Strinati, *An Introduction to Theories of Popular Culture*, 2nd edition (London: Routledge, 2004).
8. Ibid., p. 10.
9. Paul Lopes, *Demanding Respect: The Evolution of the American Comic Book* (Philadelphia: Temple University Press, 2009), p. 40.
10. Herbert J. Gans, *Popular Culture and High Culture: An Analysis and Evaluation of Taste* (New York: Basic Books, 1974), pp. vii, 3.
11. Erich Goode and Nachman Ben-Yehuda, *Moral Panics: The Social Construction of Deviance* (Cambridge, MA: Blackwell, 1994), p. 11.
12. Stanley Cohen, *Folk Devils and Moral Panics*, 3rd edition (New York: Routledge, 2002), p. 46.
13. Goode and Ben-Yehuda.
14. For an exhaustive bibliography of these studies, see Cohen, pp. xiv–xliv. See also Chas Critcher, *Moral Panics and the Media* (Philadelphia: Open University Press, 2003).
15. Mary de Young, *The Day Care Ritual Abuse Moral Panic* (Jefferson, NC: McFarland & Company Publishers, 2004).
16. Joel Best, *Random Violence: How We Talk about New Crimes and New Victims* (Berkeley: University of California Press, 1999).
17. Craig Reinarman, "The Social Construction of Drug Scares," *Constructions of Deviance: Social Power, Context, and Interaction* (1994), pp. 92–105.
18. Howard Becker, *Outsiders: Studies in the Sociology of Deviance* (New York: Free Press, 1963).
19. Cohen, p. 117.
20. *Brown v. Entertainment Merchants Association*, 08-1448 (2011).
21. Cohen, p. 45.
22. "Clinton Attacks Violent Games," *San Jose Mercury News*, April 25, 1999, p. 23A.
23. Kai T. Erikson, *Wayward Puritans: A Study in the Sociology of Deviance*, revised edition (Upper Saddle River, NJ: Prentice Hall, 2004).
24. Goode and Ben-Yehuda, p. 32 (emphasis in original).
25. Cohen, p. 58; Goode and Ben-Yehuda, p. 31.
26. Bill McCollum, "Fight Juvenile Crime," *Orlando Sentinel*, August 13, 1997, http://articles.orlandosentinel.com/1997-08-13/news/9708120450_1_juvenile-crime-violent-juvenile-juvenile-courts.
27. Barry Krisberg et al., "Youth Violence Myths and Realities: A Tale of Three Cities," National Council on Crime and Delinquency, February 12, 2009.
28. See Mike A. Males, *Framing Youth: Ten Myths About the Next Generation* (Monroe, ME: Common Courage Press, 1999). Ronald Burns and Charles Crawford, "School Shootings, the Media, and Public Fear: Ingredients for a Moral Panic," *Crime, Law, and Social Change* 32 (1999), pp. 147–168.
29. See *Roper v. Simmons*, 03-633 (2005). *Miller v. Alabama*, 10-9646 (2012).
30. See Barry Glassner, *The Culture of Fear: Why Americans Are Afraid of the Wrong Things* (New York: Basic Books, 1999).
31. Federal Bureau of Investigation, "Ten Year Arrest Trends: Totals, 1996–2005," *Crime in the United States: Uniform Crime Reports, 2005* (Washington, DC: US Department of Justice, 2005), Table 32, www2.fbi.gov/ucr/05cius/data/table_32.html.
32. Joel Best, *Social Problems*, 2nd edition (New York: W.W. Norton and Company, 2012).
33. Entertainment Software Association, Industry Facts, www.theesa.com/facts/index.asp.

2
ANTI-MOVIE CRUSADES
Fears of Immigration, Urbanization, and Shifts in Childhood

The first storefront nickelodeon opened in Pittsburgh in 1905, featuring short silent films for a nickel, attracting thousands of customers who packed into sometimes ramshackle theaters. These early movie theaters quickly multiplied in cities, particularly in neighborhoods heavily populated with immigrants and the working class. According to film historian Robert Sklar, inside the theater "one found crowds of men and women, unescorted girls and unsupervised children studying lurid posters."[1] As the movie industry grew nationally, movie theaters proliferated from an estimated 5,000 in 1906 to 20,000 in 1920.[2] "Movies were the most popular and influential medium of culture in the United States" for nearly half of the twentieth century, Sklar concludes.[3]

Just two years after the first nickelodeon opened, the Chicago city council passed the first municipal censorship ordinance against movies in the country, allowing its police department to censor or even ban films they believed a threat to public safety. Shakespeare's *Macbeth* was reportedly one of the first films to be censored. A court upheld this ordinance in 1909, presuming that the public might imitate events portrayed in a moving picture, thus granting the state the right to censor films in the interest of law and order—even films depicting actual events.[4] Why were people so concerned about these short silent films?

Many of the same reformers who thought America would be better off without alcohol turned their attention to the movies after the passage of the Volstead Act and the start of Prohibition. Activists railed against alcohol as a central source of sin and other problems; just as with alcohol, anti-movie crusaders focused on the working-class, immigrant populations living in cities. Just as Temperance movement activists feared the saloons where working-class immigrants gathered, movie theaters offered similar opportunities to congregate.[5] It was not just liquor or movies they were afraid of, it was the people they thought most vulnerable to their influence: the poor, the non-Protestant, the non-native born, the non-white, and the young. In the years to come, the new movie industry would propel many Jewish immigrants out of working-class life and into executive boardrooms. Would these newcomers forever change what it meant to be American?

An amalgam of politicians, preachers, Progressive Era activists, and members of newly empowered women's groups proclaimed themselves guardians of morality in order to "protect" others from these changes taking place. Moral crusaders argued that movies were behind the spread of vice in growing urban centers. Clergy members warned their parishioners from the pulpit of the sin movies brought, by enabling women to be in the company of men in a darkened room, by remaining open on Sunday and violating the Sabbath, for exposing children and other impressionable viewers to sex and violence, and even for instigating racial violence and threatening public safety. As with other moral crusades against popular culture, campaigns to control movies were about much more than their content: they reflect fears of social change and demographic shifts. Activists managed to get laws passed that censored and restricted movie content: they also pressured the movie industry and audiences themselves.

The belief that movies can cause social problems like crime and juvenile delinquency today has roots in the work of these moral crusaders. Their complaints preceded any social science research on the connection, and in fact likely were the primary reason that such studies were conducted at all and continue to this day.

This chapter explores how news coverage about the alleged dangers of movies framed immigrants, non-whites, the poor, and children as folk devils. Additionally, anti-movie moral crusaders—specifically the mayor of New York and religious leaders—not only used their existing power in their campaigns against movies, but also sought to gain power and status in the process. They did so at a time when immigrants and the growth of cities created demographic changes in the United States that they and others feared, and struggled against in vain. Ultimately, these demographic changes also coincided with the popularity of the movies, making movies an easy target for a moral crusade.

Scary Movie News Stories

Moral crusaders argued that movies caused violence and vice and they encouraged the public to think of movies as a cultural threat, if not for themselves then for others. While the public might not have completely bought into the idea that movies were responsible for all of the social ills, as moral crusaders claimed, by getting their claims into the news on a regular basis activists successfully planted the question about the negative effects of movies—and other forms of popular culture—for years to come.

Reformers argued that movie audiences were particularly vulnerable and potentially dangerous. According to Joseph Levenson of the Motion Picture Commission, the nation's welfare was at risk because:

> The motion picture draws an enormous proportion to its trade from children of immature years, from a great many of mental defectives, and a vast number of illiterates and the ignorant. The non-English speaking foreigners contribute great numbers to every one of these classes.[6]

"With enormous immigration of hot-headed people of several European countries crime has been on the increase," claimed the Reverend I. K. Funk in 1907, who argued that movies acted as a contagion for "persons of certain temperaments" whom he said would "instinctively imitate the crimes of others," much like a yawn might elicit a yawn from others.[7] At first foreigners, the "illiterates and ignorant," were seen as vulnerable as children, a sentiment that would fall out of favor by the mid-twentieth century as immigrant groups assimilated. But in the early decades of the century, these groups seemed to pose enough of a threat that activists warned of the dangers movies could present.

Sensationalized newspaper headlines fanned the flames as well; "Films Scare Boy to Death" (*Washington Post*, November 1, 1911), "Boy Shoots Sister: Russell Lowery 'Acted a Play' He Saw at a Theater" (*Washington Post*, March 9, 1913), "Moving Pictures Make Him Bandit" (*San Francisco Chronicle*, November 2, 1908), "Picture Show Evils Attacked" (*New York Tribune*, January 19, 1909), "Crime Taught to Youths: Evil Effect of Cheap Moving Picture Shows Described" (*Chicago Daily Tribune*, February 18, 1907), and "Panics Start Easily in 'Movie' Houses" (*New York Tribune*, February 3, 1913) were just some of the headlines warning of this new "menace."

News stories portrayed children as uniquely vulnerable to movies. In 1911, *The Washington Post* reported that a five-year-old boy in Detroit fainted while watching a movie with "Halloween hobgoblins and witches." The boy later died, which the story attributes to his being "scared to death" by the film.[8]

While arguments about protecting children are common today, this was a relatively new idea at the end of the nineteenth century. Much like today, critics charged that children would be tempted into a life of crime from films depicting lawlessness, that real-life crimes committed by youth were the result of seeing movies, and that representations of romance or sensuality would seduce young people into immorality. A 1907 *Chicago Tribune* story, "Crime Taught to Youths," quotes a sermon of a local minister who claimed that, like saloons and "gambling in cigar stores and barber shops," movies teach children "how thieves work and escape."[9] The *Los Angeles Times* called movies "schools for crime" in 1908, citing the low price of admission that "attracts a large number of children. Hence the large amount of evil that may be easily done."[10]

In 1914, three boys, one aged 9 and the other two 14, assaulted and intended to rob the younger boy's 89-year-old grandfather. The *New York Times* reported that the boys got the idea from a movie.[11] An 11-year-old boy shot his younger sister in 1913 while playing with a gun. A *Washington Post* story reported that the children had been to the movies earlier that day, suggesting that the children got the idea to play with the gun from the film.[12]

Like today, a century ago many people also argued that young people were not just vulnerable but were becoming more dangerous. These concerns coincided with an increased awareness about juvenile delinquency following the creation of the first juvenile court in Illinois in 1899; most states created their own courts by 1925. "As a highwayman or burglar, this breed of youth is the most dangerous of the present day . . . The boy crook shoots or strikes with entire abandon. He glories in it. As a rule, he does not stop at his first victim," the *Los Angeles Times* warned in late 1906.[13] "Not long ago I found boys in my school who carried revolvers," a Chicago principal told the *Tribune* the same year, claiming they did so because their screen heroes did. "The effect of these cheap shows on the school children is demoralizing. Some of the children have become so bad that they almost are incorrigible."[14] "A great number of criminals guilty of robbery, of kidnapping girls, of wild escapades in drinking and sexual debauchery, and even of murder, could truthfully say: 'We were just trying out what we have seen in the movies,'" claimed a 1922 article.[15]

Much like today, concerns about popular culture were linked with complaints about other people's parenting, particularly low-income and immigrant parents who populated the country's growing urban areas at the time. "The world is morally rotten," a minister told the *Baltimore Sun* in 1921, complaining that "the children rule the family and the family goes to the movies on the children's orders . . . Because the parents haven't the moral stamina to run things themselves."[16] "The revolt of youth against their parents and all law is principally due to the movies," sociologist Edward A. Ross told the *New York Times* in 1926. "Judges are agreed that a large share of juvenile crime is traceable to the movies," he insisted.[17]

Prevailing beliefs suggested that, like children, the poor, immigrants, women, and persons of color had more limited self-control, and were therefore more easily influenced by movies. For instance, screenings of legendary African American boxer Jack Johnson's filmed fights in the 1910s led critics to demand that they be banned, citing a threat to children. Some New York theaters specifically tried to prevent African Americans from attending screenings. "The owners of the films have been opposed to the idea of presenting [the films] in any theatre near the negro [sic] . . . quarter . . . Popular prices will not prevail, and those interested seem to think that this will discourage negro attendance."[18] Officials feared that Johnson's fights against white opponents would spur racial violence (but apparently only by blacks against whites).

Likewise, in 1928, British residents of India—then a British colony—expressed fear that American movies would have a dangerous effect on Indians and other "Oriental minds":

> The prestige of the ruling race in India is being ruined in the eyes of the Indian people by the exhibition of movies in which white men and white women are depicted taking part in scenes of . . . revolting barbarity and baseness and criminality of every description. Mob violence in which the players for the screen take part and the revolutionary plots in which they so often figure serve . . . to undermine in the Indian youth's respect for authority, and thereby the foundation upon which British rule in that country is being sapped.[19]

The notion that movies could threaten imperialism is telling of the larger fear movies triggered; groups seen as a threat to the social order, more so than movie content itself, created concerns amongst anti-movie crusaders. Critics around the world feared a new cultural imperialism of American films, which enjoyed worldwide distribution after World War I curtailed European filmmaking. Likewise, the Vatican's official newspaper criticized Hollywood films in 1927 for "offend[ing] the sanctity of Rome and the piety of hundreds . . . in the capital of Christendom."[20]

Stories like these appeared because of moral crusaders, people who argued that children, new immigrants, the poor, and people of color had more limited ability to control their emotions, that they were somehow less rational. And with immigration rising at the start of the twentieth century, moral crusaders—like the mayor of New York and religious leaders— feared that the influence of the movies on these groups could cause irreparable social harm. But what was in it for them?

Mayor and Moral Entrepreneur

The success of the 1907 Chicago movie ordinance empowered politicians such as New York's Mayor George McClellan, Jr. to further regulate the new industry, and gain political capital in the process. George McClellan—the namesake of his father, Civil War general George McClellan, Sr.—was an ambitious young mayor. Elected to his first term in 1903 at age 38, he had already served eight years in the House of Representatives and had presidential ambitions. His crusade against the movies was less fervent than many of his contemporaries, but instead likely reflected an attempt to distance himself from the corrupt Tammany machine which had put him in office—and was associated with tolerating vice—as he sought a role on the national stage.

McClellan went after the gambling and prostitution in the city despite pushback from one-time political allies. Reflecting concerns about alcohol use among immigrants by prohibitionists, he proposed limiting the number of saloons to one per thousand residents. His crackdown on vice then turned to movies, which he thought needed to be shut down to protect the public from their alleged immorality.[21]

McClellan did not view himself as a Progressive Era reformer by any means. In a speech to the Military Order of the Loyal Legion (a fraternity of Civil War officers and their descendants) he espoused his view of small government. "This passion for trying to cure all political, economic, social, moral and physical ills of humanity by legislation would be as absurd as it is futile."[22] McClellan spoke of the dangers of "general government supervision," equating it with socialism. He saw reform as "an individual responsibility" and government's primary purpose was to "maintain law and order."[23] And yet he believed he could act unilaterally if law and order or public safety were at risk.

Figure 2.1 George B. McClellan, Jr., Mayor of New York, 1904–1909

McClellan, like many of his contemporaries, likely viewed the new moving picture shows as vulgar entertainment for the uneducated.[24] Born into privilege, "his standards were those of a nineteenth-century aristocrat," according to historian Harold C. Synett.[25] In late 1908, two days before Christmas, McClellan threatened to close all of New York City's movie theaters after his visits to 30 establishments. He presided over a public hearing on the matter.

"Is a man at liberty to make money from the morals of the people?" asked the Reverend Dr. J.M. Forester, testifying at the hearing. "Is he to profit from the corruption of the minds of children?" continued Forester.[26]

"I am not opposed to moving picture shows or theaters," Canon William Sheafe Chase testified, "I am only opposed to bad moving picture shows and bad theaters." The Brooklyn clergyman would spend the next several decades lobbying against movies.[27]

A representative from the Prevention of Cruelty to Children also appeared at the hearing. "The darkened rooms, combined with the influence of pictures projected onto screens, have given new opportunities for a new form of degeneracy."[28]

Not all of the testimony supported closing down the theaters. The attorney representing theater owners reminded the mayor that Thomas Alva Edison—a highly regarded individual without "charge [of] immoral tendencies"—had himself helped to create the movies. And the president of the United States, Theodore Roosevelt, had allowed moving pictures to be taken of him, as did president-elect William H. Taft. If moving pictures were immoral, why would these upstanding men have had anything to do with them?[29]

Perhaps the strongest testimony against the ban came from Charles Sprague Smith, founder of the People's Institute, a Progressive Era organization created to support the rights of immigrants and the working class, who mentioned the importance of access to low-cost entertainment as a respite from their daily toil.[30]

"We should at the present time try to limit and control these things which are much more rotten than the moving pictures," Smith said, receiving what the *New York Tribune* described as "a prolonged outburst of applause."[31]

"If there is any such demonstration repeated I will have the chamber cleared," Mayor McClellan thundered.

Others spoke out against revoking moving picture theaters' licenses, including former city aldermen, a Lutheran deacon, and a spokesperson for the Juvenile League, a Progressive Era initiative to involve young people in city sanitation efforts.[32]

The testimony against closure appeared to do little to sway the mayor's opinion. On Christmas Eve, the mayor released his decision: "I will revoke any of these moving-picture show licenses on evidence that pictures have been exhibited . . . which tend to degrade or injure the morals of the community."[33] The city's 550 theaters were all closed that Christmas.

A court overturned McClellan's movie theater decision two days after it was issued, ordering an injunction against the license revocation. Ruling that revoking a theater's license "must not be arbitrary, tyrannical, or unreasonable," New York Supreme Court Justice Abel Blackmar concluded that the mayor's order was "not a valid exercise of . . . power."[34] Shutting down specific establishments for license violations would have been legal, but the blanket order he issued was not.

McClellan's concerns about movie theaters were not completely unfounded. Like many turn-of-the-century buildings in New York, many of them were dangerous for inhabitants. As he noted after his visit to several movie houses, "I have personally seen . . . rear exits blocked up, the doors fast, ladders missing, steps on same broken, and almost invariably a lack of lighting of the exits on the exterior after dark."[35]

The popularity of movies caused many theaters to be filled beyond fire code capacity, and film itself was highly flammable. At the time, only two inspectors worked in all of New York City, and inspections were typically announced ahead of time.[36]

After a fire at a Boyertown, Pennsylvania, opera house in January 1908, which killed 171 people who were unable to exit the building, fears of fire were amplified. Although patrons had been attending a church play, the *New York Tribune* warned readers that the same—or worse—could happen in one of the city's hundreds of movie houses:

> A cheap theater without a moving picture is a hazardous hole at best. The exits are few and small, the building is usually a ramshackle affair, and the management just as lax as the city officials will endure. Install a [film projector] and the peril is amplified tenfold . . . Should the huge rolls of picture films catch fire from any cause, or a gas tank explode, the audience would be penned in without hope.[37]

These dangerous conditions persisted throughout the city, notably in garment factories such as the infamous Triangle Shirtwaist, which went up in flames in 1911, killing 146 workers. Why were cheap amusements so high on McClellan's radar, while many other buildings were at least as likely to burn? Perhaps his opinion was swayed by the moving pictures' very vocal critics, whose fervor to stamp out the evil they believed movies contained would gain the attention of politicians at the local, state, and federal levels in the coming years.

In an attempt to mollify critics, film exhibitors decided to create their own board of censors in the spring of 1909. The board would include industry representatives as well as those from high-profile community groups. Despite industry attempts to quell critics and the injunction against McClellan's movie house shut-down, the courts generally supported restrictions on movie theaters.

Between 1911 and 1922, six states passed legislation to censor motion pictures after their dissatisfaction with the industry's board of censors. In 1915, a unanimous United States Supreme Court decision, *Mutual Film Corporation v. Industrial Commission of Ohio,* ruled that film content was not protected free speech, and therefore not subject to First Amendment protection. They argued that "theater, the circus, or movies may be used for evil" and "the exhibition of moving pictures is a business, pure and simple, originated and conducted for profit," wholly different from the press.[38] This precedent would guide movie production until it was overturned by a 1952 decision.

The Crusade Expands: Religious Diversity as Threat

And yet for some activists, particularly Canon William Sheafe Chase, Rector of Christ Protestant Episcopal Church, these laws did not go far enough. He waged a long campaign against Sunday shows, concerts, and boxing matches and in his tenure as an activist spoke out against alcohol, birth control, and books he found offensive. There is also evidence that Chase lobbied McClellan to use his authority as mayor to go after movie theaters.[39]

Chase was a quintessential moral crusader, rooting his claims as a fight between good and evil, using his position as church rector to assert his authority, and gaining status from his involvement in the moral battles he fought. All of his causes were based on what he saw as rising immorality in the culture, stemming from the growth of religious diversity and secularization of public life.

Chase maintained a sharp focus on movies, writing *Catechism on Motion Pictures in Inter-State Commerce* in 1922, where he called for federal censorship of movie content. He argued that the many municipal and state censorship boards were easily pressured by industry forces, and called for his followers to lobby members of Congress to enact new censorship laws and for federal supervision of the morals and salaries of actors.[40]

In *Catechism on Motion Pictures*—written in a bizarre Q&A style in which Chase apparently interviews himself—he argues that movies are a "new evil" and that moviegoers are "the most impressionable and weakest elements in any community."[41] Those that produce movies are "panderers of moral filth" and the "enemies of public morality" according to Chase, who makes it abundantly clear that these producers are mainly Jews, whom he sees as constituting an "evil power."[42]

Many of the new movie industry were Jewish immigrants, leading Chase and others to fear that the dominant Protestant culture would be forever changed by the new cultural power of the movies. As cities grew in the early decades of the twentieth century, restricting all activities on Sunday became increasingly difficult. Not only do Jews traditionally observe the Sabbath on Saturday, but they comprised a large proportion of exhibitors in the new motion picture industry.

"These moving picture shows on Sunday would lead to immorality," Canon Chase argued at a public hearing about Sunday licensing. Sunday laws—sometimes called "blue laws"—kept many businesses closed on Sundays until several Supreme Court decisions in the 1960s found most of these statutes unconstitutional. Today, many states still restrict the sale of liquor on Sundays.[43]

Along with Chase, a representative from the Women's National Sabbath Alliance protested granting licenses to show movies on Sundays:

> There is a desecration of our American Sabbath, largely by the foreign element who have come here to enjoy the advantage of our country . . . we refuse to let the alien and newcomer impose upon us his crude ideas of freedom.[44]

For Chase, quoted in the *Times*, "The real trouble is that the business is in the hands of a few men," whom he argues "make money by giving pictures which are below the morality of the general public."[45] Chase blamed "the anti-Jewish feeling which exists in the United States" on their failure to "petition Congress for an effective and just law regulating their business."[46] Claiming that the movies made Jewish producers extremely powerful, he feared that their "power . . . is being used for selfish commercial and unpatriotic purposes . . . to corrupt government, demoralize youth, and break down the Christian religion."[47] For Chase, limiting the influence of movies was the equivalent of stopping "the exceedingly powerful Jews."[48]

Chase even suggested that the movies themselves may be part of a larger plot by Jews, stating that "Patriotic Gentile Americans are wondering whether or not there is any race purpose in the demoralizing effects of motion pictures."[49] He cites the notorious anti-Semitic tract *The Protocols of the Wise Men of Zion*, elaborating on its claims of a Jewish plot for world domination, yet claims he harbors "no anti-Jewish spirit but a profound admiration for the real Hebrews."[50] Chase is among those referenced by Henry Ford's blatantly anti-Semitic *The International Jew: Aspects of Jewish Power in the United States*, which also concluded that "misguided leaders of Jewish religion" posed a threat to American culture.[51] Chase also openly supported the Ku Klux Klan, praising the organization in a 1922 sermon for its "devotion to maintaining the . . . ideals of the Republic . . . Personally, I think that the violent enemies of the klan [sic] are more of a menace to the public welfare."[52]

It might seem difficult, not to mention unconstitutional, for the federal government to monitor the morals and the salaries of movie stars, but this is what Chase called for. Chase's *Catechism* came in the aftermath of the first major Hollywood scandals. With the alleged profligate lifestyles of movie stars, anti-movie activists saw a new potential for a negative influence on impressionable members of the public. By the early 1920s reports of alcohol and drug use among "picture players" riled reformers, as did concerns of wanton sexuality in the new film colony out west. The 1922 murder of director William Desmond Taylor suggested affairs and other scandalous behavior among the case's many suspects. It became a widely publicized "crime of the century," garnering regular newspaper coverage.

In response, the movie industry created a new "decency czar," former postmaster general during the Harding administration and Presbyterian Church deacon Will H. Hays, who would become president of the Motion Picture Producers and Distributors of America (MPPDA), an organization that would become the main lobbying arm of the industry. Once Hays took office, no state was able to pass censorship legislation, and an attempt to create a federal censorship board also failed.

Canon Chase found a new nemesis in Hays, claiming that "the Hays organization has acted as 'a smoke screen to enable the movie trust to earn a profit from crime-inciting films,'" and once again demanded that the federal government step in and provide oversight—and investigate Hays himself.[53] Chase had testified before Congress in 1928, citing the film *Old Ironsides* (a 1926 film depicting the *USS Constitution*'s heroic role in the war of 1812) as "appeal[ing] to the gutter instincts of humanity."[54] He held rallies in Washington: 35 attended in 1928, while just 18 did in 1929, leading one of Hays' assistants to call Chase "a leader without an army."[55]

The failure of Prohibition and its eventual repeal in 1933 effectively ended widespread public support for new morality-based laws at the federal level. With that, the moral crusades of the "leader without an army" faded from public view.

The Crusade Continues: The Catholic Church and the Legion of Decency

Chase might not have had many followers, but another group would soon find more success with their anti-movie crusade. Leaders within the Catholic Church complained about film content, especially a 1927 MGM film *The Callahans and the Murphys*, which drew accusations of being anti-Irish and anti-Catholic.[56] Although anti-Catholic sentiment had not disappeared, by the late 1920s Catholics enjoyed wider acceptance than they had at the start of the century. In part, World War I offered many European immigrants the opportunity to display their loyalty to the United States, and the salience of ethnic differences began to subside for those of European ancestry. Thanks to the wave of immigration from southern and eastern Europe, the US had a larger Catholic population—20 million in 1936 compared with just over six million in 1890—who gradually gained inroads into the American mainstream.[57] Coupled with the growing number of Catholics in the population, the hierarchical nature of the Church helped organize its followers, who would soon be told that viewing a film the Church found immoral was the equivalent of a mortal sin.

Martin Quigley, a Catholic and editor of a movie trade paper, teamed with Jesuit priest Daniel A. Lord to try and "clean up" the movies. Unlike Chase and earlier crusaders, Quigley and Lord did not call for censorship or new regulations, but instead an enhanced code of movie production. Instead of a list of suggestions, a new production code— written with the cooperation of a priest and Catholic laity—would be enforced by the Hays Office before a film was even made.[58] Producers would be required to submit the script for review before filming, and the Hays Office would screen the film and recommend any changes before its general release.

"The Code," as it came to be known, did not just seek to limit sexual and violent content, but explicitly focused on issues of class and race, to "protect" those thought to be morally weak. "Passion should so be treated that these scenes do not stimulate the lower and baser element," according to part II2c. Representations of whites involved in the sex trade could not be depicted (III5), nor could "miscegenation," romantic relationships between blacks and whites (III6). Movies could not depict scenes of childbirth—even in silhouette (III8)—since activists feared that any representation of pain during childbirth might promote birth control or limit the birth rate.

The Code was also notably vague in places, leaving the door open for the Hays Office to exercise a great deal of discretion. Words like "excessive" peppered the Code, as did instructions that some things would be acceptable "only when essential for the plot." Section III of the Code states: "The treatment of low, disgusting, unpleasant, though not necessarily evil, subjects should always be subject to the dictates of good taste and a regard for the sensibilities of the audience." The Hays Office would have the power to determine what "good taste" and "audience sensibilities" would mean.

Part II of the Code insisted that "The sanctity of the institution of marriage and the home shall be upheld." Part XIII focused on religion, stating that "No film or episode may throw ridicule on any religious faith," nor could clergy members be depicted as villains. Patriotism was also part of the code: "The use of the Flag shall be consistently respectful." International relations were also to be taken into consideration, as "the history, institutions, prominent people and citizenry of other nations shall be represented fairly." Depictions of surgery, executions, or animal branding were also off-limits.

Critics of the Code argued that filmmaking would no longer reflect a broad spectrum of human experiences, but instead be reduced to simplistic fare acceptable for children. Meaningful social critiques would likely not meet the new Code's standards either. Films realistically depicting the Great Depression could be subject to censorship as "propaganda."[59]

The onset of the Depression left movie producers scrambling to maintain box office revenues. Initially Hays saw the adoption of the Code as good for marketing, but revenues fell after the Code's 1930 implementation.[60] Movies that seemed outside of the bounds of the Code did well at the box office, such as the new genre of gangster films.

The Hays Office initially worked with studios to find a happy medium in suggesting changes, which could be appealed by a jury of other studio executives.

But for anti-movie crusaders, the Code was not enough. In 1934, the Catholic Church began holding rallies protesting the continued "moral decay" in films. The Church formed the Legion of Decency, which would publically boycott films its leaders considered objectionable based on its own review board, which would assign letter grades to films. Church leaders encouraged parishioners to take a pledge not to see "unwholesome" movies. According to Paul W. Facey, a sociologist and Jesuit priest, an estimated five million people took this pledge; they were mostly Catholics, but some Protestants and Jews also participated.[61] While there is scant evidence that the boycott had a significant financial impact on box office receipts, the negative publicity was enough for the industry to act.[62] Catholics comprised a large proportion of urban populations, still central to the industry and box office profits.

The solution was to install Joseph I. Breen in the Hays Office as head of the newly created Production Code of America (PCA) in 1934. Breen was in charge of public relations for the Eucharist Congress, a massive gathering of Catholic clergy and parishioners. Under Breen, films would require a stamp of approval before their release; there would no longer be an appeals process, and studio executives could no longer overrule the decisions of the Hays Office. Refusal to cooperate could lead to a $25,000 fine (more than $438,000 in 2014 dollars).[63] Breen would amass a tremendous amount of power; he would later declare "I am the Code," and in 1941 became a studio executive at RKO (where he lasted only nine months).[64]

Breen used his authority to reinforce his own religious and political beliefs. Film scholar Gregory D. Black observed that Breen's office made sure that no films "deal[t] too directly with . . . racism, poverty, or unemployment," or challenged "militarism, fascism, or war."[65] Breen would challenge any film that seemed critical of the government, the justice system, corruption, or seemed in any way unpatriotic.[66] In the case of one film, he went as far as to censor out garbage on the street from a set depicting a slum.[67]

Despite Breen's involvement, some Legion of Decency members were still concerned about film content. The volunteers appointed to screen films, graduates of Catholic universities or convents, often disagreed about the content of different films, which they were supposed to evaluate based on the likelihood that they would lead to sin.[68]

Like Canon Chase before him, Joseph Breen's interests in enforcing the Code that controlled movie content went well beyond the films themselves but were also about *who* was making them. His written correspondence with leaders within the Catholic clergy reveals Breen's deep-seeded anti-Semitism. In a 1933 letter, he "recommended that the hierarchy form a committee to study the movie problem 'to keep the Jews worried.'"[69] The Jews in Hollywood were "simply a rotten bunch of people," Breen wrote, calling them "dirty lice" and "the scum of the earth."[70] Breen wrote that not only were Jews within the movie industry "a rotten bunch of vile people with no respect for anything beyond the making of money," but that somehow these greedy capitalists also comprised a large proportion of Hollywood communists.[71] For Breen, having power over movie production was not simply about moral purity, but also a means to exercise power over movie moguls, many of whom were Jews who had become very wealthy.

Although many of these newly minted millionaires would personify the American dream, as immigrants who became successful entrepreneurs, for some they represented a threat to the social order. No longer limited to working in the garment industry or other areas within the industrial labor machine, the fact that immigrant Jews gained wealth and influence on popular culture was clearly behind the anti-Semitic attacks of moral crusaders like Chase and Breen.

The Decline of the Anti-Movie Crusades

The power of the Code would begin to diminish after World War II, when more independent studios emerged and were less likely to worry about a Legion of Decency boycott than the major studios. Competition from television and later European movies—often far racier than American studio fare—further limited the power of a threat of a boycott and reduced the power of the Legion of Decency and other anti-movie crusades.

While concerns about movie content never completely disappeared, the level of intensity of anti-movie crusades began to ebb after World War II. The introduction of television reduced movie attendance; as the baby boom started, young suburban parents found staying home more practical.

Important legal decisions changed the cultural environment as well. The 1948 US Supreme Court decision *United States v. Paramount Pictures, Inc.* meant that movie studios could no longer hold a monopoly on film production, distribution, and exhibition. Previously, studios would require theaters to show a block of their films—known as block booking—giving exhibitors less control over which films they ran in their theaters. This opened the door for more independent studios to compete as well, many of which openly ignored the production code.

In 1952, the court decided *Joseph Burstyn, Inc. v. Wilson*, which over-turned the 1915 *Mutual* decision that concluded movies were not protected free speech. The unanimous 1952 ruling determined that movies did merit First Amendment protection. That the movie in ques-tion, *The Miracle* (1948), was an Italian film was significant at a time when European filmmaking would continue to push the boundaries of Code-era movie norms. Several cases between the 1950s and 1970s challenged the meaning of obscenity and effectively legalizing some forms of pornography, provided it does not offend "prevailing commu-nity standards."[72]

With competition from Europe, American movie-making began to change, particularly during the 1960s, as the anti-war and civil rights movements shifted the national conversation towards social criticism. Movies not only challenged the government and were sometimes criti-cal of authority figures—verboten in the Code—but also became more explicit in terms of dialogue and sexual content, including references to drug use, prostitution, and abortion.

And as the people involved in movie-making and movie viewing lost their "outsider" status, the working-class immigrants of the turn of the century became middle-class Americans by mid-century. Pro-Ameri-can propaganda films during World War II enabled studios to display their patriotism; Jewish moguls no longer seemed as foreign and, as

Jews assimilated into mainstream American society, Judeo-Christian religious diversity seemed less of a threat.[73] Jewish movie industry leaders often supported conservative anti-communist causes during the McCarthy-era red scare, expelling those named as possible communists from the industry. It wasn't just that Americans got used to going to the movies, but they got used to the *people* associated with the movies, reducing the power of future anti-movie crusaders.

Timing and Context: Behind the Anti-Movie Moral Crusades

While anti-movie crusaders argued that movie content should be controlled on moral grounds, the underlying reasons and broader social context suggest other factors influenced their passionate pleas. Rather than simply offensive movies, moral crusaders like George McClelland, Jr., Cannon Chase, and Joseph Breen were concerned about what they viewed as a substantial threat to a society's moral fiber, driven by the sense that something was changing society for the worst. While not necessarily the only causes, immigration, urbanization, and economic shifts can help us understand what helped drive the fear that movies posed a moral threat to the nation during the first decades of the twentieth century. These changes helped alter the way people thought about childhood and adolescence, which would be redefined as periods of moral vulnerability that movies supposedly threatened. As European immigrants assimilated and joined the upwardly mobile middle class after World War II, moral crusaders got less traction by focusing on them, and instead concentrated on young people as threatened by popular culture.

The America that New York City Mayor George McClellan, Canon Chase, and their contemporaries were born into following the Civil War was a dramatically different place just four decades later. Immigrants arrived in larger numbers than ever before; the foreign-born population more than doubled between 1870 and 1900.[74] For the native-born, the large number of immigrants from Southern and Eastern Europe seemed particularly alien, culturally strange, compared with immigrants of Anglo-Saxon heritage who dominated mid-nineteenth-century emigration. McClellan notes in his autobiography of the ethnic changes taking place in one New York ward. Sicilians, Neapolitans, and—as

McClellan put it—"the lowest class of Yiddish Jews" populated the neighborhood blocks from where he once lived.[75]

As the expansion of the industrial economy spurred the growth of cities, the divide between the wealthiest and the poorest not only grew but became more visible. Contentious labor strikes and violent reprisals were common—the Pullman strike in Chicago in 1896 led to 13 dead and 57 injured; also in Chicago, the Haymarket rally of 1886 demanding an eight-hour workday led to violent clashes with police. Not only did the working class challenge their working conditions, silent movies often did as well. As historian Steven Ross describes, the earliest movies often told stories of workers victimized by greedy capitalists and promoted labor-related causes.[76]

Concerns about movies didn't abate with growing prosperity following World War I and the decline of European empires. Movie theaters grew increasingly opulent and attracted more affluent customers. The boom years of the 1920s created more leisure time and discretionary spending. As sociologist Gary Alan Fine observes, the "social upheaval" taking place following the war created concerns about consumerism and self-indulgence in a period of growing wealth.[77] Fine describes how the newly created movie capital was "seen as a place of moral and physical otherness: a world devoted to conspicuous consumption."[78]

Hollywood came to symbolize all that was presumably wrong with twentieth-century America, as the United States was transitioning from a mostly rural, agrarian nation to an increasingly urbanized society; the number of people living in cities would rise to the majority by 1920. Fearing the inevitable shift in political power, Congress even refused to reapportion the House of Representatives after the 1920 census.[79]

The meaning of childhood began to shift, thanks in part to the growth of the so-called family wage, rendering child labor less necessary in some families. Low wages for adults meant that children commonly worked in the labor force. More than a quarter of all boys ages 10 to 15 worked for wages in 1900; about two-thirds of children that age worked in the agricultural industry as well.[80] While about 75 percent of 10- to 15-year-old boys living in rural areas still worked in agricultural settings in 1930, the number of boys working elsewhere for wages declined dramatically: from about one-third in 1880 to 6 percent in 1930 (girls' labor force participation rates were somewhat lower and also declined).[81] The workplace was filled with safety hazards for both adults and children, for whom agricultural work was still believed to be enriching, but reformers viewed children working in urban environments as a threat to the new view of children as innocent and in need of protection.

The notion that childhood should be a protected period of innocence was only possible when families became less dependent on children's work and wages. Viewing kids as in need of protection rather than in need of a disciplined work ethic, middle-class reformers sought to remove children from city life. Proposed child labor laws, the start of compulsory education, and the creation of a separate juvenile justice system were all part of Progressive Era attempts to reduce children's exposure to urban life.[82]

The new affluence reduced the need for child labor and created new concerns about idle youth, which would intensify even during the Great Depression, when the large proportion of unemployed people of all ages could spend more time at movie theaters, despite overall declines in admission. Children in cities who once enjoyed a degree of independence as workers found themselves adapting to new constraints as they left the labor force and entered schools in larger numbers. As historian David Nasaw writes, many young people resented their loss of freedom and chafed under the new level of supervision they found in schools.[83] These changes both reflected and reinforced concerns about delinquency, which some observers were quick to blame on movies.

Censoring movies to protect children became the rallying cry of activists; while concerns about women, people of color, and immigrants viewing movies gradually faded with the success of the civil rights and feminist movements, the danger to children argument is still popular. Groups that sought to protect children from abuse expanded their domain to also protect children from what they viewed as immorality and vice.

These complaints would echo throughout the century, as prosperity meant more leisure time for young people, and more emphasis on childhood and adolescence as times of fun. As European immigrants assimilated and anti-Semitism became less widespread, moral crusaders gained the most traction by focusing on the effects of popular culture on children and adolescents in the years ahead, particularly as young people continued their move out of the paid labor force.

Learning from Crusades Against Movies

It's a mistake to think that the explicitness of today's movies means that the anti-movie crusades of the past failed. First, they helped cement the permanence of the argument that children would imitate popular culture, setting the agenda for many future crusades that could gain attention and support by focusing on the alleged harm done to children. Second, they successfully established a precedent of pressuring industry self-regulation, which comic book, music, and video game manufacturers would all adopt in some form, by creating a ratings system. While early twentieth-century anti-movie crusaders would likely be very unhappy with today's movies, they might see the crusades against popular culture and its alleged harm to youth as an important legacy, one that would continue as the experiences of youth and social changes continued.

The movies became a site of struggle for several reasons: they were initially produced by and for groups with less social power, who were feared as a threat to native-born, mostly rural Protestants. Movies were perhaps the most ubiquitous form of popular culture, shared by the majority of Americans. In 1930, an estimated 65 percent of Americans attended at least one movie a week (weekly movie attendance has steadily declined since).[84]

Spread by sensational news stories about violence and accusations of immorality by so-called experts, the movies were a new and not yet well-understood form of popular culture, one first enjoyed by those believed to be morally weak. Moral crusaders, like politicians and religious leaders, were able to take advantage of the existing anxieties about demographic changes taking place. The working class, immigrants, and upwardly mobile Jews served as ready-made scapegoats or folk devils. That movies were first associated with them helped moral crusaders construct movies and moviegoers as potential threats.

The struggles around popular culture would shift after the anti-movie crusades, particularly as European immigrants assimilated and many of the working class experienced upward mobility after World War II. These groups would seem less threatening, but their children would continue to be a source of concern. After the end of the Depression, most of them would not be back in the paid labor force and would have much more leisure time, heightening concerns about juvenile delinquency and the forms of popular culture that were increasingly made specifically for them.

Notes

1. Robert Sklar, *Movie-Made America: A Cultural History of the Movies* (New York: Vintage Books, 1975), p. 19.
2. For 1920 data, see Filmbirth, "The History of Cinema in USA 1900–1920," www.filmbirth.com/usa.html. For 1906 data see Frederick S. Lane, *The Decency Wars: The Campaign to Cleanse American Culture* (Amherst, NY: Prometheus Books, 2006), p. 83 (see note 30).
3. Sklar, p. 3.
4. Gregory D. Black, *Hollywood Censored: Morality Codes, Catholics, and the Movies* (New York: Cambridge University Press, 1994), p. 10.
5. See Lee Grieveson, *Policing Cinema: Movies and Censorship in Early-Twentieth Century America* (Berkeley: University of California Press, 2004), p. 82.
6. "Movie Morals under Fire," *New York Times*, February 12, 1922, p. 80.
7. "Crime as a Contagious Disease," *Christian Observer*, December 18, 1907, p. 18.
8. "Films Scare Boy to Death," *The Washington Post*, November 1, 1911, p. 1.
9. "Crime Taught to Youths," *Chicago Daily Tribune*, February 18, 1907, p. 3.
10. "Schools for Crime," *Los Angeles Times*, October 13, 1908, p. 114.
11. "Robbed, as in 'Movies,'" *New York Times*, January 12, 1914, p. 11.
12. "Boy Shoots Sister," *The Washington Post*, March 9, 1913, p. 1.
13. "Five-Cent Theaters Schools of Crime," *Los Angeles Times*, December 21, 1906, p. 111.
14. "Citizens Roused by Crime Shows," *Chicago Daily Tribune*, October 6, 1906, p. 7.
15. "A Peril or an Uplift?," *Herald of Gospel Liberty*, February 9, 1922, p. 123.
16. "I've Won the Victory," *The Baltimore Sun*, February 10, 1921, p. 16.
17. "Styles the Movies 'Greatest Plague,'" *New York Times*, March 15, 1926, p. 24.
18. "Theatre Wrecked in Fight Pictures Row," *New York Times*, July 12, 1910, p. 14.
19. "Are American Movies Injurious for India?," *The Baltimore Sun*, March 3, 1928, p. 11.
20. "Films and Jazz Hit in Clean-Up in Rome," *New York Times*, April 24, 1927, p. 22.
21. George Brinton McClellan, *The Gentleman and the Tiger: The Autobiography of George B. McClellan, Jr.* (New York: Lippincott, 1956), pp. 205, 206.
22. Ibid., p. 20; "Mayor to Loyal Legion," *New York Tribune*, December 3, 1908, p. 5, http://chroniclingamerica.loc.gov/lccn/sn83030214/1908-12-03/ed-1/seq-5/;words=tried+Mc+McClellan+try+cure+passion+trying.
23. Ibid., p. 19.
24. Ibid., p. 31.
25. Ibid., p. 36.
26. "Wage War on Shows: Mayor Hears Evidence," *New York Tribune*, December 24, 1908, p. 4.
27. See also Matthew Bernstein, *Controlling Hollywood: Censorship and Regulation in the Studio Era* (Brunswick, NJ: Rutgers University Press, 1999).

28. "Wage War on Shows."
29. Ibid.
30. "Picture Shows: Better Licensing and Broad Censorship Would be Welcome," *New York Times*, January 12, 1909, p. 8.
31. "Wage War on Shows."
32. See Daniel Eli Burnstein, *Next to Godliness: Confronting Dirt and Despair in Progressive Era New York City* (Champaign, IL: University of Illinois Press, 2006).
33. "Picture Shows All Put Out of Business," *New York Times*, December 25, 1908.
34. "Moving Picture Shows Win," *New York Times*, January 7, 1909, p. 18.
35. "Picture Shows All Put Out of Business."
36. Ibid.
37. "Lessons from Boyertown," *New York Tribune*, January 16, 1908, p. 6.
38. *Mutual Film Corporation v. Industrial Commission of Ohio*, 236 US 230 (1915). Also see Black, p. 16.
39. Black, p. 12.
40. "Demands Federal Censor for Films," *New York Times*, August 28, 1922.
41. William Sheafe Chase, *Catechism on Motion Pictures in Inter-State Commerce* (Charleston, SC: Nabu Press, 2012 [1922]), pp. 8, 6.
42. Ibid., pp. 77, 15, 13.
43. "Censor for Pictures," *New York Times*, March 13, 1909, p. 1.
44. Ibid.
45. Ibid.
46. Chase, p. 115.
47. Ibid.
48. Ibid.
49. Ibid., p. 116.
50. Ibid., p. 119.
51. Henry Ford, *The International Jew: Aspects of Jewish Power in the United States* (Dearborn, MI: The Dearborn Independent, 1922), p. 157. Ford quotes Chase extensively: "He said that the Supreme Court of the United States has said that this is a Christian country and the courts in the State of New York have said that Christianity is the common law of our land . . . This government has treated the Hebrew more generously than any other nation in the world. I believe that the people generally, Hebrew as well as Christian, are very glad to enter into the spirit of Christmas time. Any attempt therefore to eliminate Christ from the hymns of our country from the reading books and from the religious holidays of the Christian people I believe is not instigated by the Hebrews as a whole but by certain misguided leaders of Jewish religion" (pp. 156–157).
52. "Canon Chase, Episcopalian, Defends Klan," *New York Tribune*, November 27, 1922.
53. "Demands Congress Sift Film Industry," *New York Times*, December 19, 1929, p. 17.
54. "Milliken Replies to Chase on Films," *New York Times*, December 20, 1929, p. 19.
55. Ibid.
56. Frank Walsh, *Sin and Censorship: The Catholic Church and the Motion Picture Industry* (New Haven: Yale University Press, 1996), p. 36.
57. For 1936 data see US Census Bureau, "Table 56: Religious Bodies—Denominations, by Number of Churches and by Membership: 1926 and 1936," *Statistical Abstract of the United States: 1940*, 62nd edition (Washington, DC: Government Printing Office, 1940), www2.census.gov/prod2/statcomp/documents/1940-02.pdf, see p. 71. For 1890 data see US Census Bureau, "Table 73: Religious Organizations—Total Number, Number of Communicants or Members, and Value of Church Property, 1890–1906, With Number of Sunday Schools, Officers and Teachers and Scholars,

1906, By Denominations," *Statistical Abstract of the United States: 1910*, 32nd edition (Washington, DC: Government Printing Office, 1910), www2.census.gov/prod2/statcomp/documents/1910-02.pdf, see p. 110.

58. Walsh, p. 61.
59. Black, p. 55.
60. Black, pp. 41, 53.
61. Paul W. Facey, *The Legion of Decency: A Sociological Analysis of the Emergence and Development of a Social Pressure Group* (New York: Arno Press, 1945), p. 57.
62. There is evidence that box office revenues declined in Philadelphia, but only for a short time. See Walsh, p. 116.
63. Black, p. 182. For inflation rate, see www.bls.gov/data/inflation_calculator.htm.
64. Black, pp. 296, 292.
65. Ibid., pp. 246, 283.
66. Ibid., pp. 246, 252, 268.
67. Ibid., p. 278.
68. Facey, pp. 66, 111.
69. Cited in Walsh, p. 87.
70. Black, p. 170.
71. Black, p. 70; Walsh, p. 157.
72. *Miller v. California*, 413 US 15 (1973).
73. See Karen Brodkin, *How Jews Became White Folks and What That Says About Race in America* (New Brunswick,, NJ: Rutgers University Press, 1998).
74. US Census Bureau, "Table 2: Region of Birth of the Foreign-Born Population: 1850 to 1930 and 1960 to 1990" (Washington, DC: Government Printing Office, 1999), www.census.gov/population/www/documentation/twps0029/tab02.html.
75. McClellan, p. 252
76. Steven J. Ross, *Working-Class Hollywood: Silent Film and the Shaping of Class in America* (Princeton, NJ: Princeton University Press, 1998).
77. Gary Alan Fine, *Difficult Reputations: Collective Memories of the Evil, Inept, and Controversial* (Chicago: University of Chicago Press, 2001), p. 140.
78. Ibid., p. 142.
79. US Census Bureau, "History: 1920 Overview" (Washington, DC: Government Printing Office, 2012), www.census.gov/history/www/through_the_decades/overview/1920.html.
80. Robert Whaples, "Child Labor in the United States," Economic History Association, October 7, 2005, http://eh.net/encyclopedia/article/whaples.childlabor.
81. Ibid.
82. See David Nasaw, *Children of the City: At Work and at Play* (New York: Anchor Books, 2012).
83. Ibid.
84. Michelle Pautz, "The Decline in Average Weekly Cinema Attendance: 1930–1960," *Issues in Political Economy* 11 (2002), http://org.elon.edu/ipe/pautz2.pdf.

3

ANTI-PINBALL CRUSADES

Fears of Gambling and Free Time

In August 1936, New York City's charismatic mayor, Fiorello La Guardia, ceremoniously dumped contraband into the Long Island Sound off of Port Washington. With members of the press present, he oversaw the dumping of thousands of confiscated weapons. Besides guns, knives, and brass knuckles, officials dumped hundreds of slot machines and pinball machines into the water.[1] The next year, the mayor presided over the dumping of more than 1,600 slot and pinball machines.[2] By 1942, when the mayor ordered every available patrol officer to confiscate pinball machines, the number seized jumped to nearly 3,000 machines.[3] Pinball would be banned in New York City from 1942 to 1976, "the longest ban in gaming history," according to the *Guinness Book of World Records*.[4]

In the midst of the Great Depression and the start of World War II, it may seem odd that La Guardia and other politicians across the country would focus on pinball at all. Today, pinball machines are relics of the pre-video game age, found at a few remaining arcades, held by collectors and even in museums. But earlier these games had filled arcades and the occasional recreation room, first attracting young men

49

and eventually drawing players of all ages. For those unfamiliar with pinball:

> The machine usually has a backboard illustrating a theme of sports, foreign places, or show girls. The game is associated with flashing lights, lurching scoreboard totals, bells, buzzers, and fast-moving player action . . . The player usually shoots from three to five balls, depending on the machine, trying to register the highest score possible on the lighted vertical scoreboard (backboard) by hitting various lights, bells, bumpers, and areas with the ball. High scoring requires keeping the ball in play on the board for the longest possible time without allowing it to go out of play through exits strategically located at the bottom of the slanted playing surface. The ball is kept in action by electric flippers, which the player activates, located at the base of the playing area and in other strategic spots. A player often tries to keep the ball in action by tilting, hitting, or jostling the machine.[5]

Pinball appeared in the midst of the crisis of the Great Depression and gained popularity during World War II and the years following the war. New pastimes that emerge during times of flux are likely to generate concern: in this case, concerns about organized crime, gambling, and the potential impact on young people. These concerns were not entirely invented out of thin air: some pinball machines did pay off in small amounts, and the all-cash nature of the game made them appealing to organized crime.

At a time when young people—and unemployed adults—had a growing amount of leisure time on their hands, cheap amusements that might now seem trivial took on greater meaning. It didn't take long for pinball to show up on moral crusaders' radar; just five years spanned between the invention of the first coin-operated machines in 1931 to their ban in Washington, DC, in 1936.[6] Described as "evil chattels" by a US attorney, most court cases hinged on whether pinball was a game of skill or a game of chance, with games of chance subject to regulation as forms of gambling. Machines that paid winners coins, tokens, balls, or even free games were likely to fall under this category.[7] From the 1930s to the 1970s, city and state governments across the country sought to regulate or even ban pinball entirely, leaving numerous state and federal court decisions in their wake.

In this chapter, we will examine how and why politicians and parents worked so hard to ban pinball. Part of a larger crusade against organized crime—which often profited from all-cash businesses—politicians sought to present themselves as tough on racketeering through enforcement of pinball bans. Their moral crusades were effective, at least temporarily, because they drew upon fears of a new game at a time of crisis as the Depression and then World War II created concerns about leisure time.

As with movies, initially it wasn't so much the activity itself that garnered scrutiny as much as *who* played pinball and where they played. Drawing large groups of young men in working-class neighborhoods seemed to pose a threat to not just the moral order, but the broader social order during the Depression and war years. Pinball often included racy images of women on the machines, and was associated with dark, smoky arcades and peep show machines. Crusaders found bars and arcades that would attract working-class, mostly male patrons unsuitable for young people who might be drawn in by pinball machines. At the time, moral crusaders thought that predominantly male spaces—like recently shuttered saloons—promoted vice and were antithetical to morality and responsibility. Men who "played" instead of worked or fought during the war could easily be characterized as folk devils.

Reformers focused much of their rhetoric on protecting children from the dangers supposedly accompanying pinball. Branded as addictive and allegedly targeted at youth who were feared to be more susceptible to the lure of pinball, reformers and some parents worried that kids would waste their lunch money and their time.[8] And, as with movies, timing and context help explain the moral crusade. Pinball became popular when the meaning of childhood and adolescence shifted. No longer needed in the labor force, young people and their growing amount of leisure time—and eventually discretionary spending—would trigger fears of growing delinquency, especially as men went off to war in Europe and the Pacific.

Besides shifts in the experiences of childhood and adolescence, gambling itself would become mainstream by the end of the twentieth century, also ushered in by the growth in leisure time and discretionary spending. Gambling began losing its sinful reputation in the twentieth century amid expanding tolerance for how people chose to spend both their leisure time and discretionary income. With the economic growth following World War II, idleness gradually lost its association with immorality as fun became commodified and sold. While it may seem quaint today, the fight over pinball served as one of moral crusaders' major battles over gambling specifically and gaming more generally, one they would lose eventually on a scale they could never have imagined in the 1930s.

The Origins of Pinball

Pinball is a game derived from the French billiard table game Bagatelle, where a player tries to get a ball past wooden pins into holes. A coin-operated version of the game, called "Baffle Ball," first appeared in Chicago in 1931. Its invention coincided with the Great Depression and provided cheap entertainment for the masses of people who suddenly found themselves with a lot of time on their hands.[9]

Because the machines were relatively inexpensive and drew patrons into small, local establishments, they proliferated quickly and, like movies, were located mainly in working-class areas of cities. At less than $20 a machine and a penny per play, it was affordable for shopkeepers and a cheap way for customers to pass the time.[10] But unlike movies, pinball didn't experience upward mobility for decades. While "picture palaces" sprung up in wealthy parts of cities and helped fuel widespread acceptance of movies, pinball remained largely sequestered in local taverns, diners, and bowling alleys for years.

The timing of pinball's invention coincided with another major historical event: Prohibition and the subsequent rise in organized crime. With Prohibition's 1933 repeal, many bootleggers and rum-runners had to find new ways of making fast money that would be hard for the government to trace and regulate. Slot machines thrived and, with many people desperate to revive their financial fortunes, gambling served as a last hope or means of escape.[11] According to one historian, "gambling surpassed bootlegging as the principal source of underworld profits" in the 1930s, with an estimated $500,000 a day coming from slots.[12] Emboldened by Prohibition-era profits and newfound power, organized crime became a major problem for cities. Struggling financially from the Depression's fallout, cities couldn't compete with payoffs the mob gave many police officers, and law enforcement corruption often allowed illegal industries to continue unabated.

Cities cracked down on slot machines, and eventually pinball machines—or "pin games" as they were sometimes called—became a new avenue for cash until they too became the target of lawmakers.[13]

Fiorello La Guardia, Moral Crusader

Like his predecessor George B. McClellan, Jr., 30 years before, New York City Mayor Fiorello La Guardia felt it was his obligation to eradicate vice from the city when he took office in 1934. Both challenged the corrupt Tammany political machine and its patronage system that skimmed the public's money (although La Guardia had never benefitted from Tammany's support, unlike McClellan).

La Guardia's view of corruption stemmed from his experience as the child of immigrant parents; he saw political patronage as a way to keep money in the hands of the powerful and city services from those who needed them the most. He considered himself the protector of the working class "little guy" struggling to get by, people he felt were often duped by the powerful.

One of those powerful forces was gambling. La Guardia thought it seduced low-income men who would spend money gambling instead of buying necessities for their families during the depths of the Depression. He thought games such as pinball were particularly pernicious. Biographer Thomas Kessner notes that La Guardia argued "these small-change games inveigled the young, leeched the poor, and corrupted the police and politicians."[14] La Guardia even held a gambling fair called "You Can't Win" to try and prevent the public from gambling in the

Figure 3.1 Fiorello H. La Guardia, Mayor of New York, 1934–1945

first place, hoping to educate New Yorkers about the long odds against winning.[15]

Much like McClellan, La Guardia saw the mayor's office as his source of unlimited power, especially if he perceived the power grab would benefit the city. Kessner describes La Guardia as bearing "combustible righteousness with a keen political sense."[16] As is often the case with moral crusaders, La Guardia felt the righteousness of his cause not only gave him the right to take decisive action, but the responsibility to do so. At one point La Guardia ordered "sanitation trucks [to] confiscate salacious magazines from street vendors under his authority to collect garbage."[17] He even went after noise pollution, directing police to target people playing radios, honking car horns, and sidewalk organ grinders.[18] His critics and colleagues alike referred to him as a "little dictator" and "little Napoleon," a reference to both his small stature and his full use of the power of the mayor's office.[19]

La Guardia's power—much like President Franklin Roosevelt's—stemmed from the city's desperation during the Depression. Coupled with a corruption scandal that forced his predecessor Jimmy Walker out of office, La Guardia had something of a mandate to provide aid during the economic crisis and dismantle the corrupt political infra-structure that had plagued the city for decades. This enabled him to take bold action on a number of issues. So while pinball wasn't La Guardia's central focus, it was part of his larger mission to eradicate gambling and organized crime. As the first Italian American mayor of New York, he took umbrage at the association of Italians with organized crime. His fight against gangsters was personal, not simply political posturing.

For his efforts, the mayor could expect some much-loved publicity, eventually becoming "the most visible and ubiquitous mayor the city had ever known," and perhaps the most visible mayor the country had known for taking on the rackets.[20] Prior to becoming mayor he was no stranger to the flashbulb. While a member of Congress a few years earlier, La Guardia demonstrated his opposition to Prohibition by call-ing a press conference and combining two legal ingredients to create beer—and then challenging police to arrest him.[21] He also went to the bottom of a coal mine during a strike in support of the workers, and appeared on a submarine during the aftermath of a naval accident. As mayor he would show up to fires, never missing the chance to have his photo taken by the cooperative press.[22] His annual contraband dump (described at the beginning of this chapter) provided a visible record of his crime-fighting efforts in the age of concern about gangsters. This was his way of showing the success of the New York City police department, particularly following the 1935 ban on slot machines.[23] After slots, pinball would be next.

Like McClellan's brief ban of movies in 1908, the courts did not always cooperate. La Guardia tried to revoke the business licenses of pinball operators after the owner of one establishment was found guilty of gambling. In early 1936, the New York Supreme Court reserved judgment, preventing the city from revoking pinball operator's licenses. The city attorney argued that "the Mayor is engaged in a life and death struggle with these racketeers," and that the licenses were initially granted under the assumption that pinball was a game of skill. According to the *New York Times*, "Investigations and prosecutions have since shown that chance is a dominating factor." The *Times* also reported that the city's police commissioner called pinball machines "gambling devices surrounded by all the evils of slot machines."[24]

For those who have played pinball, it seems unquestionably a game of skill (and as with all games, intermingled with luck). But early versions of pinball had no flippers—levers that players operated to move the ball—until 1947. Some games payed off in coins or a free game. And while many machines were independently owned by proprietors, the mob coerced some business owners into having machines at their establishments, where gangsters would subsequently collect their cash payouts.

By 1941, an estimated 11,000 pinball machines in the city each took in about $40 in cash daily.[25] This economic power meant that the industry and local retailers had more resources to fight back against the mayor's crusade. Fearing that the industry would seek a federal injunction to prevent all bans nationwide, La Guardia stepped up his battle.

With America's entry into World War II, La Guardia could frame pinball as a waste of both time and scarce materials. "In view of the current national emergency, the metals and other materials going into these machines should be utilized for defense purposes," said the mayor, who promoted seizure of these and other items he deemed contraband to be donated for the war effort.[26] Before the war, La Guardia was named the director of the Office of Civilian Defense, a position he actively lobbied for in hopes of a role in the Roosevelt administration, which possibly explained his focus on pinball's raw material.

In early 1942 La Guardia ordered the police department to confiscate the city's estimated 12,000 pinball machines before a judge could issue a restraining order.[27] Making his case, he argued:

> The pinball machine racket is a direct outgrowth of the slot machine racket, and, as was the case with its evil parent, is dominated by interests heavily tainted with criminality. There is no difference between the two rackets other than the more subtle and furtive methods of robbing the public [its $20 million profits taken from the] pockets of school children in the form of nickels and dimes given them as lunch money.[28]

A 16-year-old also testified during hearings on the matter that he skipped school to play pinball.[29]

The New York Supreme Court refused to order an injunction against the city to stop the confiscations, ruling that pinball machines were in fact gambling devices, and the raids continued.[30] In the court's written opinion, Justice Aaron J. Levy stated that:

> Distributors of [pinball were effectively] "racketeering organizations" preying upon and misleading youth . . . for their own venal aggrandizement spread their tentacles indiscriminately . . . despite the certain knowledge that the lure and incitements of their vicious contraptions will result in increased petty crime, juvenile delinquency, and even more serious crimes. Equipment of the kind here involved is in appearance quite innocent to the uninitiated and the gullible, unaware of the conniving malefactions that lurk behind it.[31]

Pinball was thus banned in the nation's largest city, as it would remain until 1976. Not satisfied with his legal victory, La Guardia continued to rail against pinball manufacturers, stating in a fall 1942 press conference:

> The main distributors and wholesale manufacturers are slimy crews of tinhorns, well-dressed and living in luxury on penny

thievery . . . They are down to the same gutter level of the tin-
horn, because of their distribution of "larceny machines."[32]

The police commissioner noted that two tons of scrap metal were sal-
vaged as a result of the nearly 5,000 machines confiscated that year. La
Guardia also asked the FBI to investigate "why pinball machine makers
can still get brass" despite the shortage of materials during wartime.[33]

Expanding the Crusade: Children and Taxes

While New York was not the first city to ban pinball, nor was Mayor
La Guardia the first public official to raise concerns about the game,
perhaps because of the publicity La Guardia was able to garner, other
politicians around the country also sought to ban pinball.

What began as a crusade against organized crime morphed into a
movement to protect children from gambling and delinquency, despite
the lack of evidence that children were the primary pinball players, or
that the machines created gamblers or delinquents. According to the
Chicago Daily Tribune, establishments with pinball machines were
effectively "hangouts for teen-age gamblers."[34]

Perry Githens, publisher of the magazine *Popular Science*, wrote in
1942 that not only is skill minimal within the mechanics of pinball, but
that the "machines hold a special fascination for children," appearing
near "candy stores and lunchrooms, near schools and playgrounds . . .
[making] pinball the child's primer of gambling." He continued, "Candy
store casinos [caused] kids—including boys from families on relief—[to
waste] money." He also claimed the game held a "demoralizing influence on children and minors," who go on to form "bad associations, are
often led into juvenile delinquency and, eventually, into serious crime,"
concluding "The American people will come to see it as a diversion far
from harmless, an amusement which costs far too much, a game which
has built a petty racket into a full-blown public nuisance."[35]

That year, a group of mothers in Darien, Connecticut, complained
that their kids squandered milk money on pinball, leading to a ban in
that city.[36] A similar group in Boston banded together to fight "civic
evils such as the pay-off pinball machines" after concerns that children

spent their lunch money on the machines.[37] "The first victims of the meanest rackets are usually the children of the community," claimed *Better Homes and Gardens*.[38] Other critics feared that children stole money in order to satisfy their "addiction" to pinball.[39]

Even in New York, the city initially concerned with organized crime, children's morality became the central argument for the ban on pinball. The city's police commissioner claimed in 1948 that strict enforcement was necessary to prevent the machines from "impair[ing] the morals of school children" and promised to crack down particularly hard on machines found near schools (although, according to the *New York Times*, he "dodged questions seeking to find out if children were playing" pinball).[40] That same year, a New York Supreme Court decision hinged on the admission from a machine distributor that he didn't want his children to play pinball.[41]

Pinball bans spread nationwide, from Washington and New York to Los Angeles and even to Chicago, the birthplace of the game. Fourteen states banned machines that paid off in free games, considered gambling.[42] Pinball was even banned from Fort Lewis army camps in 1942, although most of the machines were in the officers' clubs.[43] A "heated discussion on juvenile delinquency" led to an ordinance in Wethersfield, Connecticut, that minors under 18 must be accompanied by an adult to play pinball.[44] In Baltimore, a store owner was convicted of contributing to the delinquency of two minors, who "spent as much as $30 a day . . . playing the pinball machine for hours." The store keeper was also accused of allowing the boys to hide a makeshift weapon and buying their stolen property, but the bulk of *The Baltimore Sun*'s coverage focused on pinball.[45] In court rooms across the country, judges played pinball for the first time to decide whether or not it was a game of chance.

As sociologist Stanley Cohen notes, activists often describe their issue as a "spreading social disease," like Githens and others do above.[46] Moral crusaders also use catchy phrases ("candy store casinos," "larceny machines") to convince the public of the cause. And, most centrally, moral crusaders cast the issue as a fight between good and evil, where pinball became conflated with juvenile delinquency and the corruption of minors more generally.

But it would be taxes, not children's wellbeing, that brought pinball to the attention of Congress and the IRS, since cash revenue was easy to hide. As coin-operated games expanded in popularity, so did the government's attempts to collect taxes on their income.

In 1942, Congress passed a bill that included a $10 annual tax on "coin-operated amusement and gaming device[s]," as a way of collecting revenue to fund the war. Pinball wasn't the only device targeted; jukeboxes had become popular, as had arcade machine guns, and tabletop baseball and football games. All the time, slot machines and other gambling devices were taxed at substantially higher rates, at $200 a year.[47]

In 1954, the statute was revised to include pinball at the higher tax rate:

> A pinball machine which is so designed that the insertion of additional coins increases the chances of winning a high score and which registers free plays far in excess of the number that a person playing for amusement normally would play off, is considered to be a coin-operated gaming device. The $250 occupational tax imposed on coin-operated gaming devices by section 4461(2) of the Internal Revenue Code of 1954 applies to such a machine irrespective of evidence of actual payoffs.[48]

Walter Korpan, an Illinois proprietor, refused to pay the $250 tax on his pinball machines, maintaining that the machines were not gambling devices. His case went all the way to the Supreme Court in 1957, which ultimately ruled against him and declared that pinball machines were "coin-operated gambling machines." After this decision, local and state governments had new reason to restrict or ban pinball as gambling devices, or at least levy a special fee.[49] Writing for the majority opinion, Justice Hugo Black noted that "the case raised important questions in the administration of revenue laws." Nowhere did Black write about harm allegedly done to children or teens.

While occasional news reports would continue to describe concerns about teenagers playing pinball, by the 1950s the interest in organized crime would once again dominate discussion of pinball. A 1957 *Chicago*

Tribune story reported that, "Hoodlum moves to monopolize the 10 million dollar a year pinball machine business in Illinois have resulted in a flareup of violence" with the provocative headline "*Tribune* Looks Into the Pinball Racket; Finds Hoodlums, Violence, and Death." The following year, a story claimed that "syndicate gangsters have converted [pinball machines] to lure money from teenagers" outside Chicago's city limits, where the game was still legal.[50] Ironically, making pinball illegal, like alcohol during Prohibition, likely did more to increase the revenues of organized crime than if the game had remained legal.

Timing and Context: Organized Crime

The 1950s were marked by a fascination with crime stories, including pulp fiction, horror comics, and popular magazines such as *True Crime*. And as television entered American households, so did crime dramas. None would be as popular as live Senate hearings on organized crime, led by Tennessee's junior senator Estes Kefauver from 1950 to 1951, in what might be one of television's first reality shows.[51]

The hearings featured testimony of notorious mobsters, some pictured only from the neck down, and drew an estimated 17 million viewers; an incredibly large audience considering there were only eight million households with television sets at that time. The hearings had a larger audience than the Army–McCarthy hearings and the 1951 World Series, making Kefauver something of a celebrity. He would soon appear on the cover of *Time* and sought the Democratic nomination for president twice.[52] (Kefauver would also lead the Senate investigation into comic books, as we will see in the next chapter.)

American studies scholar Lee Bernstein describes how "the focus on organized crime in the postwar years helped define and reinforce social and economic hierarchies that were being destabilized by the rising fortunes of the white ethnic middle class." Borrowing language from the Cold War, portraying organized crime as an un-American foreign invasion reinforced the outsider status of Italian and Jewish mobsters at a time when these groups had been assimilating into the middle class and were thus harder to identify as "outsiders."[53] Kefauver insisted that people who played slot machines "finance[d] an international conspiracy that threatened American democracy."[54] Bernstein argues that the focus on organized crime also deflected the growing power of corporations and their violations.

Just as with movies, pinball became associated with the downside of American multiculturalism, reflecting a supposed threat not just to children but the culture as a whole by "outside" influences. According to Bernstein, "ethnic crime was thus seen as part of a larger pattern of immigration, urbanization, and industrialization that was taking America away from its past."[55] Cold War fears of outsiders shaped concerns about cultural infiltration.

In a time marked by fears of communism and a backlash against Roosevelt's New Deal-era programs, politicians who once advocated for social programs might be labeled as suspicious, Bernstein notes, but they could safely attack "outsiders" and expect to gain political stature, as he suggests the Kennedys and other Democrats did.[56] Going after organized crime was also a way to attack unions, as Robert F. Kennedy famously had done with the Teamsters in his battle with Jimmy Hoffa.[57]

As attorney general, Kennedy told a congressional committee in 1962 that pinball-related gambling "attracted syndicated crime" and that the law should ban interstate sales of the machines.[58] Anti-racketeering laws did eventually allow the FBI to confiscate pinball machines that gave rewards for play and thus were considered gambling devices.[59]

Politicians across the political spectrum would find that attacks on pinball could pay political dividends. Before his turn as vice-president, Republican Spiro T. Agnew spoke out against pinball at a 1966 televised news conference, claiming that pinball should be banned in Baltimore County due to "hookups with liquor licensing." He had tried and failed the year before to ban the machines, and quickly saw his political fortunes rise, from Baltimore County official to governor that same year and vice-presidential nominee just two years later.[60] Ironically, he would be forced to resign the vice-presidency in 1973 after allegations of accepting bribes. Corruption was clearly not limited to the influence of organized crime, but the intense focus on the mob and its alleged gambling tentacles helped to shift the focus away from more traditional forms of political graft, particularly if it seemed that organized crime had an interest in a game young people played.

Timing and Context: Delinquency

The onset of the Great Depression dramatically altered children and adolescents' lives: as the labor market shrank, they were out of work and stayed in school longer. For instance, in 1919 only 17 of every 100 17-year-olds graduated from high school, while by 1939 the rate tripled to nearly 51 in 100.[61] This meant that for the first time in American history, many people in their adolescent years—dubbed "teenagers" by marketers in 1941—were mostly out of the labor force during the 1930s when pinball machines first appeared.

This created anxiety about this new social group, now no longer working. What might they do with their time? What would become of them in the future without the discipline of work? While the thought of children spending more time in school and more teens attending and graduating from high school sounds like a positive turn in history, young people's lack of productivity brought suspicion about whether they would in fact be productive in the future, especially if they hung around in places where grown men might be playing pinball instead of working.

Historically valued for their labor, the belief in childhood innocence largely reflected these economic changes; the "adult" world, especially in urban centers, would be considered a threat to this newly forming notion of what childhood should be like: protected and shielded as much as possible.[62]

Teens were a newly formed "in-between" social group: not quite children, not quite adults. They would have more leisure time and eventually enjoy their own distinct forms of popular culture, which—as I discuss in later chapters—would become a key source of anxiety. Generations before, people in their teen years might have had many adult-like experiences and responsibilities, but in the new way of conceptualizing adolescence, teens were not supposed to have these kinds of experiences. So even though people in this age group had historically spent their time in much the same way adults had before, the more teens seemed to behave like adults, the more concern their behavior brought as views of adolescence shifted.

Concerns about delinquency during the Depression and war years had parallels with fears that the influx of immigrant children had brought with the earliest movies a generation before. When a group thought to be particularly vulnerable—and potentially dangerous to the social order—is associated with a new form of popular culture, moral crusades are likely to follow. Whether movies or pinball actually harmed children was immaterial: the *threat* to the newly constructed sentimentalized child or teen was enough to alarm the public.

Even if children had not yet started playing pinball in large numbers, the concern that they *could* was enough to generate concern. As legal scholar Marjorie Heins observes, laws in the name of protecting children's innocence are passed more readily, and material that might seem objectionable for children can thus become banned for people of all ages under the guise that it is harmful to minors.[63] Claiming that young people are potentially at risk—as victims or offenders—serves as a powerful tool for moral crusaders to gain sympathy for their cause, even if they have no proof of their claims. And in times of flux, fears for the future are often deflected onto young people who serve as representatives for the changing future.

And with many men gone from homes—first to find work during the Depression, and later at war—concerns about whether young people would have enough supervision emerged. This renewed focus on delinquency also reflected fears that pinball would teach young people that you can get something for nothing by gambling, discouraging hard work for a generation already thought to have it easy.

Timing and Context: Gambling

The United States shifted from rural to urban, from native-born to foreign-born, with many whose roots extended beyond Northern and Western Europe. With these changes came concerns that traditional American values would erode, values espoused by the Temperance movement stemming from the Puritan ethic of self-control, thrift, and hard work. These anxieties about cultural change can help us understand the focus on gambling and pinball.

As historian Jackson Lears writes, the tension between hard work and luck has been a central theme throughout American history.[64] Gambling in particular represents the "opposite of [self] control," providing temptation and distracting from the task of hard work and providing for one's family.[65] In a society marked by religiosity, where piety is linked with giving, not receiving, gambling led to Puritan concerns about "the corrupting effect of riches," minimizing the need for hard work and "slow, steady progress."[66] Historian John C. Burnham adds that gambling "repudiate[s] the dedication to thrift, characteristic of a population largely concerned with producing and saving."[67]

Clearly present throughout American history, gambling had been associated with scofflaws, con artists, and the lawless West. It took place in mostly male company and, as Burnham describes, gambling became associated with crime, drinking, and smoking at "gathering places for undesireable[s]."[68] Pinball's critics were quick to note that, beyond the game itself, the location and the people associated with pinball were problematic, contrasting vulnerable youth with these seedy associations.

Burnham argues that the failure of Prohibition was a turning point in the battle to legislate morality. While at first a major victory after decades of crusades against alcohol and saloons, the difficulty of enforcement, coupled with the rise in organized crime, showed how sweeping legal changes could have disastrous unintended consequences.[69] Beyond Prohibition's failure, the growth of cities and multiculturalism gradually brought more public tolerance, particularly in the aftermath of two World Wars, when millions of men spent months overseas, isolated from their families, often passing the time gambling, drinking, and smoking.

Gambling began to lose its stigma as it became a lucrative business for legitimate organizations. In 1931, the same year that coin-operated pinball was invented, Nevada legalized gambling. At a time when the state was hurting for revenue, gambling provided an opportunity to develop and market what would playfully become "sin city" and enable some involved in organized crime to exit the underworld and develop legitimate businesses. State lotteries began later, with New Hampshire starting its own in 1963 and many others following, regularly using part of the state's proceeds to fund education.[70] With the legalization of gambling in Atlantic City, New Jersey, in 1976, and the proliferation of casinos on Indian reservations in the 1990s, gambling has become a major tourist attraction around the country.

No longer a male-dominated activity, gambling came out of the shadows to become a pastime enjoyed by people across the age and economic spectrum, from churchgoers playing bingo to high rollers at luxury casinos. More recently, with the proliferation of internet gambling, it has never been more easy to access or more difficult to eliminate gambling. And with revenues at $1.7 billion nationally, states have become dependent on lotteries to make up part of their ever-shrinking budgets.[71] Gambling has mostly lost its sinful status, and so has pinball.

The Decline of the Anti-Pinball Crusade

Although raids on pinball machines and occasional concerns about their association with delinquency continued into the 1970s, the tide turned when bans ended in Los Angeles, Chicago, and New York. Starting with a California Supreme Court ruling *Cossack v. City of Los Angeles* in 1974, the court ruled that pinball was in fact a game of skill, overturning the ban in Los Angeles. The majority wrote that "no reasonable distinction exists between the pinball games proscribed by the ordinance, and such games as archery, baseball, [and] basketball."[72]

The New York City council voted to end the ban in 1976 "as a revenue-producing measure that [was expected to] bring in $1.5 million a year" through licensing.[73] Not all members were in favor of overturning the ban; in a debate the *New York Times* described as "heated," one council member stated that, "This is misguided legislation. La Guardia was right." He also expressed concern that pinball would make the city "a magnet for racketeers and racketeering in the city." When asked for evidence by a colleague, he couldn't provide any. But another council member agreed. "On the surface it appears to be an innocent sort of device. But it will bring rampant vice and gambling back to the city. The machine is easily changeable into a gambling device." The ban was overturned by a vote of 30 to 6.[74]

While the dissenting council members' concerns sounded a lot like La Guardia's arguments, New York had dramatically changed since La Guardia's 1942 ban, as journalist Tom Buckley wrote in 1975 for the *New York Times*:

> Three decades later, with the state in the lottery business, the city taking bets on the horses, pornographic films being advertised in the press and prostitutes plying their trade on busy corners, it seems unlikely that . . . if he were still around, [he] would be more than passingly indignant at the thought of legalized pinball.[75]

Despite their shift in legal status, concerns about pinball did not completely disappear. After teens loitered outside a Fairfax County, Virginia, 7-Eleven in 1977, the county prohibited any more machines from being installed in establishments with less than 5,000 square feet.[76] Palo Alto, California, limited businesses to five pinball machines that same year.[77] Also in 1977, six were arrested in a crackdown on pinball machine payoffs near Annapolis, Maryland.[78] Perhaps the most shocking report came from southern California in 1980, where a sex offender allegedly paid a 16-year-old $230 for his 5-year-old cousin, money the teen supposedly spent playing pinball.[79]

Pinball is still restricted in various locales around the world. A Toronto zoning law still on the books prohibits more than two pinball machines per establishment.[80] South Korea recently banned a game called Pachinko, a pinball-like machine with no balls or flippers, leading some Koreans to visit Japan just to play the game.[81]

Around the same time that gambling became a more acceptable form of entertainment, other mores began changing that would knock pinball off of moral crusaders' radar. The rise of the counterculture in the late 1960s made concerns about teens playing pinball seem quaint. With a greater openness about sexuality and experimentation with drugs making headlines, pinball seemed a much lesser threat. Delinquency took on revolutionary undertones, as baby boomers coming of age created a bigger wave of fear than pinball ever could. Their clothing, hair, music, and gatherings captured the covers of *Life* magazine and other major publications, as concerns about major social and cultural changes dwarfed the fears about a game.

Pinball even played a starring role in The Who's 1969 rock opera *Tommy*, where a "deaf, dumb, and blind" boy becomes something of a cult hero for his pinball prowess. The song "Pinball Wizard" reached 19 on the *Billboard* chart that year. Pinball achieved rock and roll status: edgy and yet mainstream, part of youth culture but still representative of the outcast. When Elton John covered the song in 1975, his likeness was used on pinball machines. An arcade chain's operation manager told the *Chicago Tribune* that year that "because of Elton John, and the big demand for pinball machines in private homes I'm having trouble locating enough pinball machines for our stores."[82]

Just a few years later, the dawn of the electronic age effectively put an end to the pinball panic. The first video games for home use appeared in the late 1970s, privatizing the gaming experience and removing the cash receipts from diners and arcades. While pinball was once only accessible through urban, working-class spaces, suburban families regularly purchased the new electronic games such as Atari (1977) from toy retailers. The games' location in major retail chains proved far less threatening than pinball's origins in taverns, diners, and bowling alleys. Handheld devices—such as Blip (1977) featuring a digital dot that the player would "hit" across the screen, much like on a ping pong table—served as rudimentary video games. Some of the early games were marketed as educational memory games for children, like Simon and Merlin, both first sold in 1978. As the *Los Angeles Times* reported in 1982, sales of pinball machines fell sharply from 1979, from more than 200,000 to 33,000, thanks in large part to video games. Arcade owners found that video games drew more players and were easier to maintain.[83]

From the days of penny-per-play, pinball raked in profits, but *who* profited is central to the moral crusade. When immigrant shop-owners and suspected mobsters were the main beneficiaries, pinball was a source of worry. In 1976, a new family-oriented pizza restaurant featuring arcade games opened in San Jose, California, helping again to reshape pinball's image as safe for children. Chuck E. Cheese's became a franchise within two years, opening family-friendly arcades around the country. The free market trumped concerns about sin.[84]

Video games would certainly attract the attention of moral crusaders, as noted in Chapter 1, but for different reasons. No longer was gambling or wasting lunch money a core concern, nor did organized crime presumably pose a threat to young people playing video games. The games, in effect, went legit. Concerns about imitating violence would come later, but in their earliest incarnation, video games like Space Invaders and Pac-Man would not draw the fear that kids would imitate the games as their descendants would a few years later.

The internet further privatized "sin," making it harder if not virtually impossible to regulate. "The Internet put the anonymous consumption of vices literally at the world's fingertips," writes Radley Balko in the libertarian magazine *Reason*. "Vice, taboo, and subversion abound on the Web, often beyond not only the gaze of prying eyes but the grasp of prohibitionists," he concludes.[85] Playing games and gambling are no longer largely the domain of seedy taverns, diners, or even family-themed arcades. Pinball is no longer seen as a problem, in part because moral crusaders have moved on, but also because the spaces of its location are no longer sites of worry. Nor are the mostly middle-aged players playing a game from their youth. Pinball, ironically, has become a source of nostalgia, representing a seemingly more innocent and wholesome past.

Learning from the Anti-Pinball Crusade

The struggle over pinball had very little to do with the game itself, but was about how and where people spent their leisure time, especially when they started having more leisure time. As the labor force changed, at first expelling many adults during the Depression and many young people for good, pinball was under fire for appearing to undercut the value of hard work and to promote an underground market.

The moral crusaders could rally against pinball using existing fears of organized crime and attach those fears to young people's alleged decline in morality, which certainly didn't originate with the invention of pinball, but could be stoked nonetheless. The mob seemed especially virulent if they could be characterized as trying to lure the young with a game; moral crusaders could then argue they were protecting the nation's youth and gain political advantage.

The pinball folk devils go well beyond the manufacturers of the game or the proprietors who had machines. It's not clear how much of a role that organized crime actually played in the business of pinball, but by highlighting the threat of ethnic minorities, many of whom were recent immigrants and easily categorized as outsiders, this made it possible for what now seems like a harmless game appear to be part of a larger threat. Pinball emerged during a time of economic flux, when people had more free time, first because of the Depression and later due to postwar prosperity. Young people would be among the first to have more free time, and concerns of how they spent that leisure time would echo for the rest of the century. As we will see in the next chapter, young people would come under further suspicion during the prosperous postwar years, as would the games they played and the comics they read.

Notes

1. "Criminals' Arsenal to be Sunk in Sound," *New York Times*, August 3, 1936, p. 34.
2. "Gangster Weapons Dumped in Sound," *New York Times*, August 6, 1937, p. 36.
3. "Mayor Asks Speed in Pinball Raids," *New York Times*, January 25, 1942, p. 32.
4. Guinness World Records, www.guinnessworldrecords.com/records-6000/longest-ban-in-gaming-history.
5. Peter K. Manning and Bonnie Campbell, "Pinball as Game, Fad, and Synecdoche," *Youth and Society* 4 (1973), pp. 333–358.
6. Edward Trapunski, *Special When Lit: A Visual and Anecdotal History of Pinball* (New York: Doubleday, 1979), p. 5; "Firm Defies DC Pinball Ban," *The Washington Post*, July 9, 1936, p. X1.
7. "Firm Defies DC Pinball Ban."
8. "Pinball Machines Get College Role," *New York Times*, October 10, 1942, p. 17.
9. Trapunski, pp. 2, 5–6.
10. Ibid., p. 6.
11. Stephen Longstreet, *Win or Lose: A Social History of Gambling* (Indianapolis: The Bobbs-Merrill Company, Inc., 1977), p. 20.
12. Thomas Kessner, *Fiorello H. La Guardia and the Making of Modern New York* (New York: McGraw-Hill, 1989), p. 351.
13. Longstreet, p. 22.
14. Kessner, p. 352.
15. H. Paul Jeffers, *The Napoleon of New York: Mayor Fiorello H. La Guardia* (New York: Wiley, 2002), p. 194.
16. Kessner, p. xii.
17. Ibid., p. xv.

18. Jeffers, p. 191.
19. Kessner, p. 381.
20. Jeffers, p. 267.
21. Ibid., p. 115.
22. Ibid., pp. 125–126.
23. Kessner, p. 363.
24. "Pinball Decision Reserved by the Court," *New York Times*, January 24, 1936, p. 11.
25. Kessner, p. 363.
26. "'Politician' Linked to Pinball Games," *New York Times*, December 28, 1941, p. 25.
27. "Mayor Asks Speed in Pinball Raids."
28. "Pinball as 'Racket' Fought by Mayor," *New York Times*, January 29, 1942, p. 21.
29. Ibid.
30. "City Wins Twice on its Pinball Ban," *New York Times*, February 12, 1942, p. 25.
31. Ibid.
32. "Mayor's Ire Turns on Pinball Machines," *New York Times*, October 17, 1942, p. 17.
33. "La Guardia Asks FBI to Probe Pinball Brass Consumption," *New York Times*, May 18, 1942, p. 2.
34. "Finds Pinball Gaming Boom Outside City," *Chicago Daily Tribune*, August 16, 1958, p. 9.
35. Perry Githens, "Plenty of Traps for Pin Money Plungers," *The Sun* (Baltimore), April 5, 1942, p. SM12.
36. "Mothers Cause Darien to Ban Pinball Machines," *The Hartford Courant*, October 29, 1942, p. 22.
37. Laura Hadock, "Boston Starts 1957 with 332 Pinballs," *The Christian Science Monitor*, January 5, 1957, p. 2.
38. October 1957 issue, cited in Trapunski, p. 98.
39. Trapunski, p. 96.
40. "First Arrest Made in Pinball Drive," *New York Times*, March 8, 1948, p. 1. "Pinball 'Racket' is Sifted in City," *New York Times*, March 14, 1948, p. 76.
41. "Pinball Objection Cited," *New York Times*, June 22, 1948, p. 27.
42. Trapunski, p. 105.
43. "Pinball Machines Banned at Fort Lewis," *The Christian Science Monitor*, July 23, 1942, p. 3.
44. "Parent, Spa Owner Fined Under Pinball Ordinance," *The Hartford Courant*, April 11, 1952, p. 22.
45. "Storekeeper Gets Two Years, Fine in Case of Juveniles," *The Baltimore Sun*, April 6, 1956, p. 26.
46. Stanley Cohen, *Folk Devils and Moral Panics*, 3rd edition (New York: Routledge, 2002), p. 46.
47. See *United States v. Korpan*, 354 US 271 (1957).
48. Internal Revenue Service Revenue Ruling, Rev. Rul. 60-102, 1960-1 C.B. 555, www.charitableplanning.com/document/668519.
49. George Favre and Emilie Tavel, "Massachusetts Lid Slammed on Pinball Gambling Machines," *The Christian Science Monitor*, October 16, 1959, p. 2.
50. "Finds Pinball Gaming Boom Outside City," *Chicago Daily Tribune*, August 16, 1958, p. 9.
51. Lee Bernstein, *The Greatest Menace: Organized Crime in Cold War America* (Boston: University of Massachusetts Press, 2002), pp. 48, 61.
52. Ibid., pp. 61–62, 67.
53. Ibid., pp. 178, 66, 70–71.
54. Quoted in ibid., p. 67.
55. Ibid., p. 25.
56. Ibid., p. 10.

57. Thomas Reppetto, *Bringing Down the Mob* (New York: Henry Holt and Company, 2006), p. 61.

58. "Committee is Told How Pinball Machines Click," *The Hartford Courant*, January 17, 1962, p. 6C.

59. Theodore W. Hendricks, "Judge is Given Pinball Lesson," *The Baltimore Sun*, November 6, 1965, p. B20.

60. "Pinball Tie with Liquor Board Seen," *The Baltimore Sun*, March 21, 1966, p. C20.

61. No. HS-21. Education Summary—High School Graduates, and College Enrollment and Degrees: 1900 to 2001, www.census.gov/statab/hist/HS-21.pdf.

62. See Viviana Zelizer, *Pricing the Priceless Child: The Changing Social Value of Children* (Princeton, NJ: Princeton University Press, 1985).

63. Marjorie Heins, *Not in Front of the Children: "Indecency," Censorship, and the Innocence of Youth*, 2nd edition (New Brunswick, NJ: Rutgers University Press, 2007).

64. Jackson Lears, *Something for Nothing: Luck in America* (New York: Viking Books, 2003), p. 2.

65. Ibid., p. 190.

66. Ibid., pp. 23, 176, 3.

67. John C. Burnham, *Bad Habits: Drinking, Smoking, Taking Drugs, Gambling, Sexual Misbehavior and Swearing in American History* (New York: New York University Press, 1993), p. 169.

68. Ibid., pp. 150–151.

69. Ibid., pp. 20–21.

70. Ibid., pp. 161–162.

71. "Lottery Payouts and State Revenue," National Conference of State Legislatures, Washington, DC, 2008, www.ncsl.org/issues-research/econ/lottery-payouts-and-state-revenue.aspx. Data are for 2006, the most recent year for which statistics are available.

72. *Cossack v. City of Los Angeles*, 11 Cal.3d 726 (1974), www.leagle.com/xmlResult.asp x?page=6&xmldoc=197473711Cal3d726_1685.xml&docbase=CSLWAR1-1950-1985&SizeDisp=7.

73. Edward Ranzal, "Council Approves Pinball Measure," *New York Times*, May 14, 1976, p. 33.

74. Ibid.

75. Tom Buckley, "It's Still the Devil's Game," *New York Times*, April 4, 1975, p. 18.

76. Caryle Murphy, "Fairfax Limits Installation of Pinball Machines," *Washington Post*, February 15, 1977, p. C5.

77. "Pinball Machine Ban," *Chicago Tribune*, May 4, 1977, p. 10.

78. "Arunel Seizes 6 in Pinball Pay-Offs," *The Baltimore Sun*, April 27, 1977, p. C2.

79. "Child, 5, Sold for Pinball Spree, Rescued," *The Hartford Courant*, April 9, 1980, p. 4B.

80. Jessica Smith, "Toronto Pinball Prohibition Defeats Illegal Pinball Café," *Metro News*, December 10, 2013, http://metronews.ca/news/toronto/472791/toronto-pinball-prohibition-parkdale-bar-ban-defeat-illegal-pinball-cafe.

81. Andrew Miller, "Korea's Ban on Pachinko Pinball Gambling Sees an Increase in Gamblers Coming to Japan," *Rocket News* 24, March 8, 2013, http://en.rocketnews24.com/2013/03/08/koreas-ban-on-pachinko-pinball-gambling-sees-an-increase-in-gamblers-coming-to-japan.

82. Jon Van, "Pinball Machines Break the Sin Barrier," *Chicago Tribune*, February 5, 1976, p. W1.

83. *Alan Citron*, "Pinball—the Industry Goes 'Tilt,'" *Los Angeles Times*, December 10, 1982.

84. For more discussion, see "An Empire of the Obscene" in Eric Schlosser, *Reefer Madness: Sex, Drugs, and Cheap Labor in the American Black Market* (Boston: Houghton Mifflin, 2003), pp. 209–210.

85. Radley Balko, "The Subversive Vending Machine," *Reason*, June 2010, pp. 60–61.

4

ANTI-COMIC BOOK CRUSADES

Fear of Youth Violence

A frenzy about juvenile delinquency took place in the years following World War II. Historian James Gilbert notes that "the growing sensitivity to the misbehavior of youth took place in a general context of heightened attention to young people . . . [as] part . . . of the public response to the new teenage culture that emerged during and after World War II."[1] As a generation came of age in a time of prosperity with more leisure time—and the beginning of niche marketing of popular culture—stories of violent youth created a wave of fear that young people were becoming a danger to themselves and others.

Ultimately, these structural changes would help usher in cultural changes, with new media such as comic books, the expansion of the magazine market into satire and pornography, and later the advent of television. Would anything go in a time of expanding entertainment media, or could the government effectively control content in the name of protecting children? Would "good taste" trump free speech and the free market?

During the 1940s, more people would read comic books than watch movies, listen to radio, or read traditional magazines, which would make this new pastime ripe for moral crusaders.[2] Read by children, teens, and young adults, newsstands featured a variety of comic genres, ranging from animal stories and Biblical tales to superheroes, romance, crime, and horror for 10 cents an issue.

Fears that comic books caused juvenile delinquency eventually led Congress to convene hearings in 1950 and again in 1953, providing committee co-chair Senator Estes Kefauver an opportunity to reprise his starring role in national headlines. And yet no reliable evidence could substantiate whether a rise in youth violence even existed, nor would any be available for two decades, until 1974 legislation led to the creation of the Office of Juvenile Justice and Delinquency Prevention and regular data collection. Before that time, national estimates on youth crimes were limited at best, but that did not stop moral crusaders from claiming that comic books threatened the safety and morality of American youth.

One of the critics' chief concerns about comic books was that they would replace more traditional reading and create a dependence on visual entertainment. Complaints about comic books would echo moral crusades of the past; not only are there similarities to complaints about movies and pinball machines, but concerns about comic books bear a striking similarity to complaints about "dime novels" from the late nineteenth century. In the 1880s, so-called "dime novels" about Western adventures, tales of outlaws, and crime stories worried critics that young people—working-class young people in particular, who were still expected to be economically productive—would waste their time, learn slang, and become morally corrupt and criminal.

Nineteenth-century moral crusader Anthony Comstock "lobbied strenuously to suppress cheap fiction."[3] Founder of the New York Society for the Suppression of Vice, and later postal inspector, in 1873 Comstock successfully pushed for a law that made sending material deemed "lewd" or otherwise "obscene" through the mail a crime. The so-called Comstock Law made selling crime stories potentially illegal if they were deemed lascivious. The Comstock Law also made sending any information about sex—including health and birth control information—a crime. He deemed dime novels "evil reading" and— along with parents, teachers, and clergy members—tried to get boys to stop reading them, much as moral crusaders would with comic books decades later.[4]

This chapter examines why both comics and young people seemed menacing in an era, ironically, often considered an age of innocence today. Comic books could be easily purchased, traded, and shared with little supervision or adult control and often featured dark stories that challenged postwar optimism. The number of comic books proliferated at the same time as concerns that unsupervised youth would get into trouble, as young people continued to exit the labor force.

Unlike crusades against movies and pinball, moral crusades against comic books began with widespread concern, started by intellectuals concerned about this new "lower" form of literature. Literary critics and journalists would also complain about a new medium that used language in a nontraditional—and seemingly threatening—way. The initial moral crusaders would not be politicians, but parents, educators, clergy, and law enforcement, who interacted with young people on a daily basis and saw comic books in children's hands. Rather than a top-down led crusade, leaders would emerge largely in response to existing complaints from grassroots groups. Their cause would later be taken up by a senator and a psychiatrist who would gain national attention as their complaints about comic books were televised.

Yes, some comics graphically depicted the macabre, and some included highly eroticized stories that parents might not have wanted their children to see, and comic book creators bore a large share of crusaders' ire. But young people themselves were increasingly seen as folk devils, no longer just considered victims but potential killers. Ironically, the fears about juvenile delinquency in the postwar era would make for an excellent comic book plot, where seemingly innocent middle-class suburban youngsters turn on those around them, as in the 1956 film *The Bad Seed*, where an angelic-looking girl kills for no apparent reason. And, like a comic book, the melodrama of the story is entertaining but not representative of most children of the era, who were perhaps the first generation of Americans to have few economic responsibilities and ample leisure time, what we now regard as time to "just be kids."

The Origins of Comic Books

Like pinball, comic books first appeared during the Great Depression as collections of newspaper comic strips. Widely read in an era where popular culture was just beginning to be marketed to a segmented audience, sales of comics increased briskly during the Depression when little else did.[5] Its 10-cent cost was affordable to many children, who could then trade or resell them to peers, or even keep them hidden from disapproving adults.

While the first books sold in 1933 were basically newspaper marketing ploys, by 1937 nearly 150 distinct comic book titles appeared.[6] That same year Detective Comics—or DC Comics for short—began, publishing mostly superhero comics, most notably *Superman* in 1938 and *Batman* in 1939.[7] The superhero comics represented a shift from newspaper comics, which comic historian Les Daniels describes as becoming "increasingly feminized" during the 1920s and early 1930s, with strips like *Blondie* (1930) focusing on domestic life and *Tarzan* (1929) increasingly about the romance between Tarzan and Jane.[8]

Comic strips date back to the nineteenth century, when the penny presses competed for working-class readership. At a time when many new immigrants weren't proficient in reading English—and many native-born Americans had limited literacy—the comics were a way of broadening the base of newspaper buyers.[9] Newspaper comics were not without controversy, particularly after the first color pages appeared in 1893 and the infamous "Yellow Kid" comic was in the middle of the circulation wars between William Randolph Hearst and Joseph Pulitzer (and thus the phrase "yellow journalism" came to deride overly sensationalized stories with little substance).[10]

When the war ended, sales of superhero comics declined, leading producers to shift their focus to crime and horror comics, which sold briskly.[11] In 1946, only about 3 percent of comic book titles focused on crime, growing to 9 percent the next year and 14 percent in 1948.[12] To be sure, some of these comics were shockingly graphic, with images of severed heads and detailed stories of killings. Comic book titles like *Crime SuspenStories*, *Tales from the Crypt*, *Crime Illustrated*, and *Violent Crime* became popular, featuring covers with illustrations of people under attack and men lying in pools of blood, as well as frequent appearances of scantily clad women.[13] Many had a particularly dark and macabre tone, similar to the work of Edgar Allan Poe. Although superhero comics typically involved good triumphing over evil, this wasn't always the case with crime or horror comics. These stories often portrayed the dark side of postwar domesticity, with some plots focusing on violence between intimates or family members.[14]

Intellectual Critics: The Origins of the Moral Crusade

One of the first public critiques of comic books was in 1940, when literary critic Sterling North wrote an editorial, "A National Disgrace," for the *Chicago Daily News*. "One million dollars are taken from the pockets of America's children in exchange for this graphic insanity," he wrote, going on to blame comics for placing "strain on young eyes and young nervous systems," the "crude" color used "spoil[ing] the child's natural sense of color," and for the "injection of sex and murder," which he argued "make the child impatient with better, though quieter stories."[15] His solution: parents and teachers should provide children with alternative stories that draw attention away from comics. The next year, *Parents* magazine called comics "a threat to character development," as observers feared that children would read comic books instead of classic literature.[16]

Even Superman wasn't immune to critique. The superhero known for protecting "truth, justice, and the American way" and who became the star of multiple television series and at least a half-dozen feature films drew criticism from those who saw similarities with philosopher Friedrich Nietzsche's concept of *"übermensch,"* or superman, roughly interpreted as man being a god on earth. To literary critic Walter Ong, writing for *Time* in 1945, Superman bore striking similarity to a Nazi (despite being created by two Jewish American men).[17] "The 'comics'. . . are furnishing a pre-Fascist pattern for the youth of America through emulation," wrote North in 1941.[18]

Was Superman's physical superiority a reflection of Adolph Hitler's master race? Did his ability to singlehandedly solve ordinary citizens' crises lend support for a totalitarian leader, or at the very least make readers complacent and expect that a savior will take care of peoples' needs?

The Catholic Church published criticisms of superheroes, deriding hero worship as a form of paganism that was akin to fascism, clearing the way for a totalitarian state. A 1943 article in *Catholic World* criticized the supernatural themes, and that heroes "defy natural laws."[19] Psychiatrist Fredric Wertham complained that Superman's ability to fly and leap over tall buildings violated the laws of physics, misleading children.[20]

North's editorial set the stage for the public debate about comic books that would last for at least 15 years, leading Parent Teacher Associations (PTAs), law enforcement agencies, and even the US Senate to take action. In cities and towns across the country, comic books would be banned, burned, and—like pinball—become the subject of numerous court hearings, particularly when news accounts attempted to make sense of youth violence by connecting incidents to comic books.

Case Studies in Crime: Triggering the Moral Crusade

A pair of high-profile incidents of youth violence would bring national attention to comic books. Did comic books make children kill children?

In October 1947, seven-year-old Lonnie Fellick's body was found after he went missing in the Chicago area. A schoolmate, 12-year-old Howard Lang, first told investigators that Fellick had been lured into the woods by three others, and police announced they were looking for a "sex criminal."[21] Lang later confessed to the murder of the younger boy, which became a sensationalized case garnering national coverage.

Turning 13 that December, the *Chicago Daily Tribune* reported that Lang would be the youngest defendant ever tried for murder in Illinois. Noting that the boys "might well have been taken for another Tom Sawyer and Huckleberry Finn," coverage frequently noted how otherwise childlike Lang and his schoolmates appeared. A boy who testified at the trial said that Lang killed Fellick to prevent him from "snitching" to his mother that Lang stole $10.[22] In his confession, Lang said he beat

Fellick for calling him "three rotten names when I wouldn't give him a cigaret [sic]."[23]

Lang originally pleaded not guilty due to temporary insanity, and his attorney planned to put teachers on the witness stand to testify that the boy was mentally unstable. Included in the defense was his unstable home life, as his mother had been married five times. But he changed his plea to guilty, saying, "I'm scared. I'm sorry I did it. I wish it hadn't happened."[24] Lang was sentenced to 22 years in the state penitentiary, and the judge blamed his mother for their "unsavory home life."[25] The Illinois Supreme Court later reversed his conviction on appeal that Lang did not understand the severity of the charges against him; he was retried and found not guilty. He later assaulted a boy who testified against him and was sentenced to a year in prison.[26]

Nowhere in the original description of the case are comic books mentioned—not by Lang, not by his attorneys, nor by the district attorney. At a sentencing hearing, Lang did mention that he liked comic books, along with mystery movies.[27] This was clearly a case of a troubled boy with significant behavior problems and a single mother unable to cope with him.[28] He also had learning difficulties; although he was 13, he was only in the fifth grade. A month after pleading guilty, Lang's attorney asked the judge to consider a movie Lang recently saw, *Born to Kill*, a factor in the case, which the judge denied.[29]

And yet some news accounts of this case focused on the alleged danger of comics. "Public concern over the contribution of crime comics to juvenile delinquency was aroused here last spring by the Howard Lang case, in which a 13-year-old devotee of such comics was indicted for murder of a seven-year-old playmate," the *Christian Science Monitor* reported, omitting all details about Lang's troubled history in a story about the formation of a citizen's advisory committee on comic books.[30] "Public castigation of the 'horror comics' in connection with the Howard Lang case is welcome grist to the mill of those educators who are striving to counteract the detrimental influence of such publications," the *Monitor* also wrote.[31]

Other cases of youth violence were likewise tied to comic books, if for no other reason than the perpetrator was young and young people often read comics. Through connecting "a succession of juvenile crimes that have apparently been prompted in some degree, at least, by the reading of the so-called 'comics,'" the *Monitor* also presents a "solution": a ban on the sale of comics, as some cities had done.[32]

When 14-year-old Roy Adams was convicted of suffocating his 8-year-old neighbor, the *Monitor* linked the cases to each other and to comic books. "The Adams boy . . . blamed comic books and association with older companions for contributing to his misdeeds."[33]

Adams, also from the Chicago area, had a history of behavioral problems, having once been "an inmate of the Parental school," a detention facility he was sent to by order of the juvenile court.[34] He initially claimed that he killed his younger neighbor because of "a spat over comic books" but later confessed to sexually assaulting the girl before killing her.

The *Chicago Daily Tribune* reported that Adams was a "husky problem boy" who did poorly in school, was prone to lying, and "was abusive." "Separate psychiatric tests had indicated that young Adams should be kept under constant supervision," the *Tribune* reported.[35] He was also present three years earlier when a six-year-old boy drowned, which was initially ruled an accident. Once in jail Adams was very uncooperative, at one point flooding his cell by stopping up the toilet and refusing to be interviewed by a psychiatrist.[36]

Like Lang, Adams was clearly troubled, with a number of factors likely contributing to his disturbing behavior. And yet the *Hartford Courant*, reporting on his conviction, ran the headline "Comic Book Fan, 14, Convicted of Murder."[37] These cases, troubling enough on their own, take on an even more menacing tone if it seems that otherwise normal, well-adjusted boys committed these gruesome acts on their "playmates." At a time when childhood was being redefined as a time of innocence and leisure, one wholly different from the struggles of the Great Depression and World War, youth violence seemed all the more shocking when it did occur.

Moral Crusaders: Teachers, Law Enforcement, Clergy

Around the same time as these shocking murders, educators, law enforcement officers, and other leaders claimed that comic books were an important cause of delinquency, and that delinquency was a new and growing problem. In a 1947 *Christian Science Monitor* article titled "Delinquency Traced to Four Potent Causes," the superintendent of the National Civic League named movies, comics, alcohol, and cigarettes as important causes of juvenile crime.[38] Rather than a new movement, crusaders against comic books were likely the same people who had already mobilized during crusades against movies and pinball. Sociologist Paul Lopes argues that the "general movement of censorship around obscenity and anti-Americanism" was in place at the time, ready to respond to comics having already focused on censoring books in the 1940s.[39]

Outraged by content, the national PTA called comic books a "menace to our children," and that their creators had "abused the public trust," and in 1948 created a resolution calling for further studies and reviewing committees.[40] The dean of Fordham University's school of education called comic books a "cancerous growth" that "ruined eyesight . . . and bred juvenile delinquency."[41]

A Baltimore bishop railed against comic books, citing examples of recent youth crimes allegedly inspired by comic books:

> Many of these new publications are most objectionable and most harmful. Teachers, psychiatrists, juvenile court officials and others dealing with the problems of the young are most positive in their statements concerning the baneful effects of many of these publications; to their influence they ascribe a considerable part of the present-day juvenile delinquency.[42]

Some law enforcement officers agreed; a resolution at the 1947 annual convention of the Fraternal Order of Police declared that comic books are "one of the contributing factors to the cause of juvenile delinquency," and that the books were "detrimental to the youth of this nation" and "the nation's mothers were helpless to protect their children from the 'lurid' booklets."[43]

Earlier that year the Pennsylvania Chiefs of Police Association drafted a resolution condemning comics, claiming "murder and assault are condoned" within their pages.[44] PTA groups across the country also rallied against comics; a Chicago PTA member called them "evil forces" that "contribute to juvenile delinquency."[45] Educators told the *Christian Science Monitor* in 1948 that comics were a "menace to the morals of the nation's youth."[46] Schools in New York City hosted debates where students could argue for or against the comics.[47] A group of students at a Catholic school in upstate New York burned comic books at a highly-publicized bonfire in 1948.[48] That same year, the Canadian Parliament banned all crime comic books.[49]

Everyday citizens voiced their concerns about comic books as well. "Bad reading . . . drives out good reading," a parent wrote in a letter to the *Hartford Courant*, complaining that children "are doping over the comics."[50] "It is not by happenstance that so many juveniles get in trouble with the law," another reader wrote in the *Courant*, explaining that "the younger generation has yet to learn self-control."[51] Another letter writer called comics "time wasters" and "breeders of juvenile delinquency."[52]

Not all professionals believed in the comic book menace. In response to the rise in news coverage about delinquency, sociologist Henry D. McKay stated that "delinquency data are so inadequate and inexact that anyone can find what he wants for whatever purposes he has in mind," and that "the talk about increasing juvenile delinquency is . . . bunk."[53] Paul Tappas, also a sociologist, said that those who blamed comics for delinquency engaged in "scapegoatism" and an "oversimpli-fication," describing the focus on comics as "one of the main fallacies blocking effective treatment of juvenile delinquency."[54] The executive director of the Society for the Prevention of Crime described blaming comic books a "twentieth century scapegoat" enabling well-meaning individuals to "run away from the real issue," which he saw as prob-lems within families.[55] Some newspapers' editorial pages concurred. "Reformers are trying to place the blame everywhere but in the right place," stated the *Chicago Tribune* in reference to the "comic book tangent."[56]

The Crusade Expands: Politicians Respond

Following the outcry of clergy, parents, police, and educators, politicians soon responded. While few took on active roles as moral crusaders, politicians across the country began proposing restrictions on comic books in their communities. On the national level, Congress held three hearings focusing on juvenile delinquency within a 10-year period, helping to create the appearance that they were taking action to stop a new and growing problem.

In 1948, cities across the country acted to ban comic books they found objectionable. A Los Angeles County supervisor noted that "these so-called comic books are so obviously detrimental to the welfare of children that immediate steps must be taken to prevent the continued sale."[57] That April, Detroit banned the sale of 36 titles within its city limits after "censors termed the books corrupting to youth."[58] Indianapolis soon followed, as did Chicago, setting up a censor board and fining those convicted of "selling or exhibiting an 'indecent or lewd book, picture, or other thing of immoral or scandalous nature.'"[59] The *New York Times* reported that by October nearly 50 cities had created bans and set up censor boards to decide which comic books to outlaw.

Newspapers around the country recognized that a new wave of censorship might not be in their best interest, as beneficiaries of free speech. The *Hartford Courant* editorialized that "some day parents will realize that the responsibility for bringing up their children is theirs . . . If your child reads dirty comic books, you should be ashamed." The editors concluded that "reading suggestive or obscene material is only one expression of human weakness. Take away all such material and the same weakness will find another poison to absorb." While not specifically condemning censorship, they note that "it's impossible to root out sin."[60]

No fan of comics—the *Courant* ran many anti-comic stories and had previously called comic books an "intellectual opiate" that "violate[s] the tenets of good taste" and a "cancer which is eating at the vitals of young America"—the newspaper both condemned comics and questioned the legal response many cities had taken.[61] The *Chicago Tribune* admitted that comic books "are frequently moronic and bloodthirsty," but argued that "their critics should prove that they actually cause juvenile delinquency," and that "there is no reason to believe that anyone ever committed a crime because of reading a book."[62]

It appeared that the political pressure had worked. In response, some comic book publishers dealt with the bad press by creating a self-regulating content code in July 1948. The Association of Comics Magazine Publishers (ACMP) consisted of 12 out of 34 publishers, who agreed to avoid presenting criminals positively or law enforcement negatively. "Details and methods of a crime" were to be avoided too. Obscenity, torture, "obscene language," and nudity or hyper-sexualized images would also not get a seal of approval under the new self-imposed rules.[63]

The code cast a wider net than just sex and violence, like the Hays Code regulating movies did a few decades prior. The comics code banned "ridicule or attack on any religious or racial group" and forbade presenting divorce as "glamorous or alluring."[64] Comics with the seal of approval were not to "lower the moral standards of those who read them" in an effort to "hold their business within the rigid lines of good taste" like the movies.[65] The editors of the *Hartford Courant* applauded the move as "encouraging" that some publishers were "willing to do something about the disgraceful situation," although they conclude that "a more thorough [clean up] may still be in order."[66]

To enforce the code, the industry hired a New York attorney, Henry E. Schultz, to run the ACMP in hopes of creating a parallel to the Hays Office: one that would both regulate comic books and fight off attempts at new legal restrictions. But the comic book industry would not find the same success. First, only a minority of publishers participated; for those that did, the review process was costly for publishers.[67] The new organization could not prevent lawmakers from passing new legislation, but the publishers would benefit from favorable court decisions the next year.

In 1949, 14 states proposed laws to regulate the sale of comic books to minors.[68] The year before, the US Supreme Court struck down a New York law that "prohibit[ed] distribution of a magazine principally made up of news or stories of criminal deeds of bloodshed or lust" as overly vague and a violation of the First Amendment.[69] Responding to public outcry, the state legislature continued to pass similar restrictions on sales of comic books. New York's proposed legislation would have had the biggest impact, since nearly every comic book was published within the state. Twice the legislature passed bills, and twice they were vetoed by Governor Thomas Dewey on the grounds that they would likely be ruled unconstitutional. Other states' bills would meet similar fates.[70]

The *New York Times* editorialized that "many people are deeply concerned over the moral and social effect of this flood of pulp paper that has been loosed on the newsstands" may be having, "but it is a dangerous invasion of freedom of the press, with which all freedoms are joined, to set aside for governmental pre-censorship one form of publication."[71]

The government would continue to consider its role in the comic book industry, responding to the incoming tide of complaints. In 1950, as part of its investigation into crime in the United States, the Senate took a closer look at the role of comic books.

Estes Kefauver: Moral Entrepreneur

As I discussed in the last chapter, the US Senate formed a special committee on organized crime in 1950, and held highly publicized hearings that year and the next. Headed by ambitious freshman Senator Estes Kefauver, these hearings would propel him into the national spotlight, and lead to a book deal and numerous television appearances—and even an Emmy in 1952 for "outstanding public service on television." Kefauver's interest in comic books was significant but fleeting; he was not exactly a dedicated moral crusader on this issue, condemning comic books' presumed role in causing delinquency as part of his larger move towards the national stage.

His critics claimed that the crime subcommittee hearings were purely platforms to "provide himself with a forum from which to seek publicity" in his presidential bids.[72] But it is too simple to say that Kefauver was simply a self-serving politician, seeking publicity through riding the wave of a moral panic. While there is no doubt the hearings catapulted him into headlines and onto the lucrative lecture circuit, he was more than just an opportunist, seeming to be genuinely concerned about crime in the US.

Figure 4.1 Estes Kefauver, Democrat from Tennessee, served in the Senate 1948–1963

And yet Kefauver's ambitions could be served by getting involved in the comic book panic. He had only recently been elected to the Senate in 1948. A New Deal Democrat, Kefauver often took positions that made him unpopular with other southern Democrats, like voting for anti-poll tax legislation and refusing to sign the "Southern Manifesto" in support of school segregation. He also weathered charges of being soft on communism by voting against bills that would curtail civil liberties. His organized crime hearings challenged some of the Democratic Party's machine politics and cost him valuable allies. Despite his popularity and national name recognition, he failed twice to earn the Democratic presidential nomination (although he was the vice-presidential nominee in 1956).[73]

While the Senate hearings mainly focused on organized crime, they also briefly addressed juvenile delinquency and comic books. FBI director J. Edgar Hoover testified that juvenile crime had "leveled off" in the postwar years, and that he would not predict "an appreciable decrease in delinquency would result if crime comic books of all types were not readily available to children."[74] The committee also solicited input from child guidance experts and public officials, such as probation officers, prison officials, and psychiatrists, whose responses led the committee to conclude that comic books were not a major contributor to delinquency. The *New York Times* wrote that:

> Time and again it is said that anti-social acts spring from no single factor. The easy inference is that the sort of thinking that is always attributing delinquency to a single cause is more harmful than helpful in the exploration of the complex of causes that forms the base of the delinquency problem.[75]

For a little while, complaints about comic books quieted down, but Kefauver found his political star was rising. After the original report on juvenile delinquency came out, Kefauver discovered that some of the child guidance experts surveyed had earned money as consultants for comic book publishers. The Child Study Association of America, whose members had worked with the publishers, countered that the consultants had helped make some comic book content more suitable for children; the individual members in question argued that they made no secret of their association. Kefauver said that the consultants "deceived the public" and the investigation was reopened.[76]

Public pressure was also a likely factor in the next set of hearings. PTA groups and members of law enforcement continued to express concerns about comic books and delinquency. By 1950, the industry code created in 1948 was all but meaningless. The cost of having each comic book screened by the ACMP meant a major expense for publishers. According to journalist David Hajdu, "emboldened by delusions of immunity, comic-book makers allowed the horror and suspense comics of the early 1950s to grow even more gruesome and lurid."[77]

In 1953, a new Senate subcommittee was formed to investigate juvenile delinquency. Comic books would be a central part of the next round of hearings. While initially New Jersey Senator Robert

Hendrickson was the subcommittee chair, Kefauver replaced him as chair the next year when the hearings took place. The subcommittee spent three days on comic books; April 21–22 and June 4, 1954. Witnesses included child psychiatrists, cartoonists, comic publishers, distributors, sellers, and the ACMP's comic book "czar" Henry E. Schultz.

Their testimony provided an array of views on whether comic books are the cause of delinquency. In perhaps the most memorable part of the hearings, Kefauver held up an issue of *Crime SuspenStories* featuring a woman's severed head on the cover while questioning its publisher, William Gaines. Kefauver asked Gaines if he believed the cover was "in good taste"; Gaines suggested that it could have been worse. Kefauver peppered Gaines with questions regarding his earnings and business practices ("Why do you have five corporations?") as well as questions of whether particular comic book plots were in "good taste."[78]

Hendrickson concluded that "not even the Communist conspiracy could devise a more effective way to demoralize, disrupt, confuse and destroy our future citizens" than crime-laden comic books.[79] In a report issued the following year, the subcommittee concluded that "this country cannot afford the calculated risk involved in feeding its children, through comic books, a concentrated diet of crime, horror, and violence."[80] The report notes in its introduction that the subcommittee recognizes the importance of the First Amendment and "has no proposal for censorship." The report also does not directly blame comic books for delinquency:

> Delinquency is the product of many related causal factors. But it can scarcely be questioned that the impact of these media does constitute a significant factor in the total problem . . . The behavioral sciences are as yet far from exact. Therefore, it is not surprising to note some diversity of opinion even among experts in the fields of criminology, psychology and sociology. Responsible observers of the American social pattern are in general agreement that juvenile delinquency has many causes, not just one.[81]

Figure 4.2 Kefauver held up this 1954 issue of *Crime SuspenStories* during the Senate Subcommittee Hearings on Juvenile Delinquency that year. Cover of *Crime SuspenStories* vol. 22, Apr/May 1954. Art by Johnny Craig Copyright © 1954 William M. Gaines, Agent, Inc., reprinted with permission. All rights reserved.

After the hearings, the comic book industry once again promised to regulate itself through a stricter code in the fall of 1954. First, no comic book would use the word "terror," "horror," or "crime" in its title. As with the 1948 code, the new code reiterated that stories should not provoke sympathy for criminals or disdain for law enforcement or any other "established authority." Good would "triumph over evil" in their stories. "Stories dealing with evil shall be used or nor shall be published only where the intent is to illustrate a moral issue and in no case shall evil be presented alluringly nor so as to injure the sensibilities of the reader." Women were to be "drawn realistically without exaggeration of any physical qualities" (the code did not address how men were to be drawn). Even advertising in the back pages would have a code, focusing on ads that likely appeared in many other magazines. "Advertisement of medical, health, or toiletry products of questionable nature are to be rejected," the code advised. [82]

In essence, the comic book industry not only promised to change their content, but somehow tried to assure the public that they could control their readers' interpretations. Charles F. Murphy, a New York City judge, was named head of the new Comics Magazine Association of America (CMAA) and would be in charge of making sure that magazines with the seal of approval met the code's standards. Twenty-four of the 27 publishers agreed to join the CMAA. Gaines, the publisher Kefauver confronted with the decapitated image on the comic book cover, decided to stop publishing horror and terror comic books altogether. (He would later turn his attention to publishing *Mad* magazine).

Some were appeased. "It's Wonderful!" exclaimed the editorial page of the *Christian Science Monitor*. "American parents, certainly, will wish Mr. Murphy and the new organization every success."[83] In 1956, Kefauver reported that "the comic book situation has been brought under control by voluntary compliance with the code of ethics," effectively ending his involvement in the anti-comic book crusade.[84] He was busy with other endeavors; that year he sought the Democratic Party's nomination for president, and then became the party's vice-presidential candidate, ultimately losing both bids.

Not all critics were happy with the new code. Psychiatrist Fredric Wertham, who testified at the subcommittee hearing that comic books were detrimental to children—especially to otherwise normal, well-adjusted children—was still convinced that comic books posed a serious threat to children and the society as a whole.

Fredric Wertham: Moral Crusader

German-born psychiatrist Fredric Wertham had become a mainstay in the public critique of comic books and was a key witness during the 1954 Senate hearings. Perhaps coincidentally, his book *Seduction of the Innocent*, which laid out his case against comic books, was published just as the hearings began. He was not impressed by the industry's new code, and in *Seduction* he wrote of his displeasure with the results of Kefauver's 1950 crime hearings and their conclusions about comic books; he was also very unhappy about what he viewed as Kefauver's abandonment of the comic book issue.

Wertham had previously written books about violence, drawing from case studies of children apparently under his care. He had practiced at Johns Hopkins Hospital in Baltimore before becoming the senior psychiatrist at Bellevue in New York, and later practiced at Queens Hospital. He also opened a psychiatric clinic in Harlem and had been one of the few white psychiatrists who would treat African Americans.[85]

Magazines such as *Colliers, The Saturday Review of Literature, Reader's Digest* and *Ladies' Home Journal* covered Wertham's complaints about comic books or published his articles or excerpts of his work. His status in the field of psychiatry and colorful commentary drew lots of attention and added gravitas to the anti-comic book crusade.[86]

For instance, after *Wonder Woman*'s 1941 debut, Wertham complained that she promoted homosexuality (as he thought Batman and Robin's partnership did too). Created by a social psychologist as a superheroine girls could admire, Wonder Woman lived in "Paradise," a land without men, and frequently came to men's rescue. She was specifically focused on revealing the futility of war at a time when war threatened much of humanity.[87]

During a 1948 speech in Boston, Wertham argued "just as we have ordinances against the pollution of water, so now we need ordinances against the pollution of children's minds." According to Wertham, comics "suggest criminal or sexually abnormal ideas," and "they create for young readers a mental atmosphere of deceit, trickery, and cruelty," and that comics "are literally courses in crime, crime primers for children!" He also argued that "comics" are a misnomer, and a better term for them would be "bloodies."[88]

He told correctional officers attending a convention that same year that comics were "literally correspondence courses in crime, crime primers for children!"[89] Wertham dismissed the idea that delinquency was declining (which we will explore later in this chapter). The *New York Times* reported that "despite statistics to the contrary, [Wertham] believed juvenile delinquency was increasing and growing in brutality. He attributed much of the increase to comic books" in an article misleadingly titled "Juvenile Delinquency Seen on Increase."[90]

In his testimony before the Senate, Wertham was given a significant block of time to recite his credentials and a prepared statement about comic books before responding to questions. In his statement he asserted that reading comic books with violence would ultimately change the moral reasoning of young readers and "cause a great deal of ethical confusion":

> If the children see these kinds of things over and over again, they can't go to a dentist, they can't go to a clinic, they can't go to a ward in a hospital, everywhere they see this where women are beaten up, where people are shot and killed, and finally they become, as St. Augustine said, unconsciously delighted.[91]

Wertham testified that young people had become significantly more sadistic and violent since comic books became popular, and he also suggested a link between comic books and teen pregnancy. *Seduction of the Innocent* elaborated on these ideas, purportedly drawn from cases of violent juveniles Wertham had worked with in his practice.

Noted sociologist C. Wright Mills wrote a glowing review of *Seduction* in the *New York Times*, saying that "all parents should be grateful" that Wertham wrote this book and that "studies of the effects of comic books on children at various age levels, on an adequate statistical basis" should be undertaken.[92] Not all reviews were positive. Robert S. Warshow wrote in *Commentary* that, although he wished his son weren't an avid fan of comic books, Wertham's tone and claims were overwrought:

> Dr. Wertham's world, like the world of the comic books, is one where the logic of personal interest is inexorable, and *Seduction of the Innocent* is a kind of crime comic book for parents, as its lurid title alone would lead one to expect. There is the same simple conception of motives, the same sense of overhanging doom, the same melodramatic emphasis on pathology, the same direct and immediate relation between cause and effect. If a juvenile criminal is found in possession of comic books, the comic books produced the crime.[93]

In its review, the *Washington Post* affirmed its disdain for comic books, but seconded Warshow's characterization of the book.[94] Some scholars argued that Wertham's research itself was deeply flawed and his book was a polemic disguised as research. Early on, sociologist Frederic Thrasher charged that *Seduction of the Innocent* did not provide a systematic analysis of comic books or delinquency. He had used a small sample, used no control groups, and included no endnotes documenting his sources.[95]

In 2010, Carol L. Tilley, a professor of Library and Information Sciences, reviewed Wertham's notes and personal papers and found even more serious problems with *Seduction of the Innocent*. She writes that he claimed to have firsthand knowledge about specific cases noted in the book, but his copious notes revealed "edited and altered children's statements" and failed to credit others when he borrowed their ideas.[96]

By comparing his notes to the book, Tilley found that Wertham selectively excluded information that would complicate his claims. For instance, in claiming that *Batman and Robin* promoted homoerotic

fantasies, he quoted two boys who were already openly gay and in a rela-
tionship with one another, although he left this detail out of the book.[97]
Perhaps the most serious charge Tilley levels is that "Wertham falsified
statements" and "fabricated the context . . . [and] conflated comments"
of the cases he describes.[98] She concludes:

> *Seduction of the Innocent* is filled with examples . . . in which
> Wertham shifted responsibility for young people's behavioral
> disorders and other pathologies from broader social, cultural, and
> organic physical contexts of these children's lives to the recre-
> ational pastimes of reading comics . . . Wertham's book appears
> clearly to be an attempt at cultural correction rather than an hon-
> est report of scientific inquiry.[99]

Perhaps Wertham's convictions about comic books led him to overstate
his case; while his methods may seem suspect today, they reflected the
popularity of psychoanalysis at the time. Within the field of psychiatry, Wertham was unique in looking more closely at social factors that
contribute to violence beyond individual psychopathology. He also
considered the role that racial inequality played in violence, a rare perspective at the time, and provided important testimony in the landmark
Brown v. Board of Education case. Wertham also testified on behalf of
Ethel Rosenberg, who was eventually convicted and executed for trea-
son, and treated her children for several years after. He was clearly a man
who felt passionately about the causes he cared about.[100]

With the growth of mass media, other scholars began thinking critically about the role popular culture played as propaganda, particularly
after the rise of fascism in Europe. As a German-born immigrant, Wertham likely had concerns about potential societal shifts that mass culture
might produce, leading to his almost alarmist tone about their danger.

And while he had a very successful career in psychiatry before
comic books, by speaking out and writing a book for a mass audience, Wertham gained access to the life of a public intellectual, one
that he clearly sought out.[101] At the dawn of television, being in the
public eye meant recognition at a whole new level. It also brought a

new medium of concern, giving Wertham and others a new cause to campaign against.

Timing and Context: Fears of Delinquency, Freedom of Expression

The anti-comic book crusades provide insight into postwar changes in conceptions of adolescence as well as the growth of entertainment media. As the Cold War began, anxiety about young people's physical, emotional, and intellectual wellbeing ran high: could this generation face the challenges presented by the dawn of the nuclear age? The red scare added an element of suspicion about dangerous subversive infiltration of communism and sabotage. Hajdu writes that comics were considered "a peril from within."[102] In a new kind of conflict—one over ideas, fought by spies and scientists—the battle over ways of thinking and fears of mind control meant that any form of popular culture could seem threatening. Significant Supreme Court decisions would also challenge old mores about "good taste" and broaden the interpretation of the First Amendment to include more graphic content in popular culture. The growth of popular culture targeted specifically at children and teens was relatively new, a change that felt invasive and threatening, and end-run around the traditional authority of parents, teachers, and clergy.[103]

Economic growth after World War II meant that most families no longer needed their adolescent children to be in the paid labor force. This, coupled with the growing need for a more educated workforce—and more scientifically savvy population for defense industry jobs—meant that more adolescents would attend high school than not.[104]

This lies at the heart of mid-century fears of delinquency. Youth "were the harbingers of a new society," argues historian James Gilbert:

> And adults were prepared to punish the messengers . . . to avoid the message that the family was rapidly changing, that affluence was undercutting old mores, that working women were altering the sexual politics of the home and the workplace.[105]

Adolescents would have an experience unlike any generation before them: with time and a little bit of money to spare, it was easy to grow concerned about youthful mischief and worse. Carried over from the absence of fathers during the war, young boys in newly created suburbs spending leisure time seemed troubling. Historian John Springhall notes that comics "invaded the sanctity of American suburbia" and challenged "the romantic idea of childhood innocence."[106] The biggest fear of moral crusaders was that comics would lead their readers to imitate its sometimes violent content, providing "courses in crime," and would be a threat to public health and safety and corruptors of youth.[107]

Delinquency rose to the forefront of popular discussion after World War II, with the popular assumption that it was getting worse. But was it really?

Since 1930, the Federal Bureau of Investigation (FBI) has gathered national crime statistics for its Uniform Crime Reports (UCR) on the most serious forms of violent and property crimes. Data collected before 1960 are generally considered less reliable than today, as fewer law enforcement agencies participated and reporting practices then were less consistent, so national trends from that time are less clear than they are today. Earliest data include only those arrested and fingerprinted. To be counted in national statistics, the fingerprint cards had to be sent to the FBI. Perhaps the most stable measure of juvenile crime is the proportion of juveniles of all those arrested that the FBI had fingerprint cards for.

According to FBI data, the proportion of those arrested who were juveniles rose during World War II, and began declining after the war ended. Between 1943 and 1945, juveniles under 18 comprised about 10 percent of all of those arrested and fingerprinted. But the FBI sounded the alarm, saying in the 1945 Uniform Crime Report this decline was likely a "leveling off," and that "until the amount of delinquency on the part of youths is reduced at least to pre-war levels, we will continue to have a situation constituting a grave threat to the future strength of our Nation."[108]

That percentage of juvenile arrests fell to less than 5 percent between 1947 and 1951, lower than it had been before the start of the war. Ironically, this drop happened at the same time that stories about the alleged danger of comic books reached its zenith. In 1952—the year FBI data collection procedures changed—the percentage of juvenile arrests did grow, from just under 8 percent, to 11 percent in 1956.[109] (The vast majority of these arrests were for property crimes such as burglary, theft, and vandalism, not for violent offenses.)

Gilbert analyzed the number of news stories published about juvenile delinquency mid-century, finding that they rose during World War II, declined immediately after, and spiked during the mid-1950s. He suggests that these stories, coupled with the "instrumental opinion" of politicians and those nominated as experts, enhanced the public's concern that delinquency was on the rise.[110] Actual crime increases don't necessarily match the *fear* of youth crime waves, bolstered by well-publicized comments by influential people.

But most people weren't then—and aren't now—aware of crime statistics, even when reliable data are available. Reading about the juvenile delinquency and comic books regularly in the news can be enough to scare readers into thinking that a problem really exists, and that something should be done.

Concerns about delinquency can create a vicious cycle: the more young people are treated as serious threats, the more likely they are to be arrested and charged rather than informally sanctioned for lesser offenses. This elevates arrest statistics, which in turn purports to show an increase in delinquency—even if young people's behavior itself is basically unchanged.

Delinquency came to mean more than just youth crime, but any undesirable behavior that failed to conform to middle class expectations. As Hajdu writes, modes of dress, dance, slang, and even a bad attitude constituted delinquency in the eyes of the public.[111] Gilbert concludes that the growing segmentation of youth culture itself felt scary and different, as it appropriated "cultural symbols and raw materials from working class, ethnic, and racial subcultures, modern youth culture sported language, music, customs and behavior that appeared to contradict middle class aspirations."[112]

It was not just the violence of comic books that upset critics, but the way in which comic books often challenged notions of happy, postwar domesticity. In crime and horror comics, family life was a site of danger, not safety. As Daniels argues, "In a medium where fantasy was the standard fare, the crime comics exposed some unpleasant truths about our society."[113] Just as film noir hits of the era featured the dark underbelly of American life, many comic books challenged the narrative of the boundless optimism of suburban life: the idea that all would be well after victory in war, the triumph of consumer capitalism, and the notion that happy families would sell capitalism's success around the world.

Comic book creators "expressed in their lurid panels . . . a disregard for the niceties of a proper society, a passion for wild ideas and . . . a cynicism toward authority of all sorts."[114] In short, such stories challenged what historian Bradford W. Wright called "a bland consensus vision of America" through comic books' implicit "criticism [of] American institutions, authority figures, and middle-class mores." Comic books, at least initially, were untamed compared with other forms of media and "stood apart from virtually every source of information and entertainment available to young Americans in the early 1950s."[115] Thanks to the Hays Code, movies had been sanitized, and comic books would soon follow thanks to the 1954 code, which all but ended horror comics.

These new forms of entertainment brought into question the definition of obscenity and the limits of free speech. The US Supreme Court would grapple with the question of obscenity just as publications like the Kinsey Reports on sexual behavior (1948, 1953) and *Playboy* (1953) would challenge social mores.

The landmark decision *Roth v. United States* (1957) upheld that content that "appeals to the prurient interests" of the "average" adult could be banned, but not content solely deemed harmful to minors. In 1973 the standard was revised in *Miller v. California* from content "utterly without socially redeeming value" to material lacking "serious literary, artistic, political, or scientific value."[116] Previously banned books (such as *Lady Chatterley's Lover* and *Tropic of Cancer*) could now be sold, as literature was no longer confined to stories appropriate for those of all ages.

As leisure time and entertainment choices expanded, so did the kinds of stories told to increasingly segmented audiences. As the business of mediated entertainment grew, so did complaints about content being violent, overly sexual, and disrespectful to authority. Rather than solely a reflection of a cruder, crueler society, the shift in content represents the growth of the entertainment market and attempts to appeal to increasingly narrower audiences.

Decline of the Anti-Comic Book Crusades

The 1954 code did not put all comic book publishers out of business, but many people lost their jobs after the industry shrank. "Between 1954 and 1956, more than half of the comic books on the newsstands disappeared," Hajdu writes; artists and writers found themselves not just out of work, but on the defensive about their earlier careers after all of the negative attention their industry received.[117] Comic books became tamer, focusing more on romance, and according to Daniels, "forced into essentially infantile patterns" to avoid the ire of their critics. In his estimation:

> The best comic books probe the subconscious . . . free from the burden of respectability [and provide] an opportunity to explore the wild dreams and desires which seem to have no place in our predominantly rationalistic and materialistic society.[118]

While horror comics began to fade in the US, British readers got their first taste of American comic books in the early 1950s, leading to a similar—although much abbreviated—panic in the UK in 1954. Their concerns mirrored those of American moral crusaders, with the added issue of American cultural imperialism, leading to legislation the next year and the concern quickly fading.[119]

The threat of violent and sexual content as well as social criticism abated in comic books, at least for a time. Comic books and later graphic novels would experience a resurgence with the 1960s counterculture; in 1970 a group of 300 fans met in San Diego for what would be the first Comic-Con, growing to about 130,000 fans in the 2010s.[120] Computer technology in the 1990s and later the internet enabled nearly anyone to create and distribute their own comics.

Television would take the place of comics for complaints about violence, and later sex. In 1950, there were about six million television sets in the United States; by 1960 that number increased tenfold.[121] As programming segmented from targeting a mass audience to targeting specific age groups, critics became increasingly concerned about its effects, drawing attention away from comic books.

Learning from the Anti-Comic Book Crusade

Comic books were a visible manifestation of the many changes taking place in the postwar era: they became a pastime of choice for young people with more leisure time, their content at times shocking as freedom of expression expanded and niche markets began to shrink. The thin booklets could be easily hidden from parents and other authority figures during a time when concerns about youthful misbehavior became characterized as ominous signs of delinquency and criminality. Unlike movies and pinball machines, which were enjoyed in public, comic books could be read in private and were harder to monitor.

And unlike movies and pinball machines, the moral crusade against comic books was more of a bottom-up process, begun by literary critics, and then by clergy, educators, law enforcement, and parents after hearing disturbing stories of youth violence. As the number of children reading comic books grew, so too did the fears that these readers would become violent as the seemingly "innocent" young killers had. Crusades against comic books were about attempts to regain authority when the expansion of children's leisure time made this more difficult. Politicians responding to the groundswell of concern were able to appear to be doing something about the perceived crisis, at least until court decisions made banning content on the grounds that it was potentially harmful to minors illegal. As television ushered in new opportunities for people to become nationally recognized figures, the potential for moral crusaders to spread their message increased. Television also provided incentives for politicians and others to crusade against something the public was already concerned about and gain national attention.

In the postwar era, children's role as economic producers shifted towards being consumers, increasing their purchasing power and the scrutiny placed on their tastes. With more time to spend reading comic books came growing concerns about who they would become in a time of rapid social change, making them—and comic books—easy for adults to fear. The handful of cases of violent youth could be generalized to all young people because they likely shared an interest in comic books, seeming to justify increased regulation of both children and comic books.

As comic book readers grew into adolescence and young adulthood, the music many would listen to would "[add] the sound track to a scene created in comic books."[122] Rock and roll would pick up where comic books left off, creating a new challenge to the social order, integrating the airwaves and turntables around the nation.

Notes

1. James Gilbert, *A Cycle of Outrage: America's Reaction to the Juvenile Delinquent in the 1950s* (New York: Oxford University Press, 1986), p. 39.
2. David Hajdu, *The Ten-Cent Plague: The Great Comic Book Scare and How it Changed America* (New York: Farrar, Straus and Giroux, 2008), p. 5.
3. John Springhall, *Youth, Popular Culture and Moral Panics: Penny Gaffs to Gangsta-Rap, 1830–1996* (New York: St. Martin's Press, 1998), p. 73.
4. Ibid., pp. 73, 170.
5. Ibid., p. 121.
6. Hajdu, p. 34.
7. Les Daniels, *Comix: A History of Comic Books in America* (New York: Bonanza Books, 1971), p. 11.
8. Ibid., p. 6.
9. Hajdu, p. 9.
10. Daniels, pp. 2, 10.
11. Amy Kiste Nyberg, "William Gaines and the Battle over EC Comics," in Jeet Heer and Kent Worcester (eds.) *A Comic Studies Reader* (Jackson, MS: University Press of Mississippi, 2009), p. 58.
12. Hajdu, p. 110.
13. Randy Duncan and Matthew J. Smith, *The Power of Comics: History, Form and Culture* (New York: Continuum, 2009), pp. 37–38.
14. Daniels, pp. 63–64.
15. Sterling North, "A National Disgrace," *Chicago Daily News*, May 8, 1940.
16. "Comics' Effects on Youth Scored," *New York Times*, November 6, 1941, p. 25.
17. Bart Beaty, *Fredric Wertham and the Critique of Mass Culture* (Jackson, MS: University Press of Mississippi, 2005), p. 115; Hajdu, p. 81.
18. "The Antidote to Comics," *National Parent–Teacher Magazine*, March 1941. Cited in Hajdu, p. 44.
19. Hajdu, pp. 79–81.
20. Carol Tilley, "Seducing the Innocent: Fredric Wertham and the Falsifications that Helped Condemn Comics," *Information & Culture: A Journal of History* 47, no. 4 (2012), p. 401.
21. "Sex Criminal Hunted for Slaying Missing Boy, 7," *Chicago Daily Tribune*, October 30 1947, p. 1.

22. Rita Fitzpatrick, "Tells How Boy Slew Pal, 7," *Chicago Daily Tribune*, February 19, 1948, p. 1.
23. Rita Fitzpatrick, "Act to Plead Lang Guilty," *Chicago Daily Tribune*, February 21, 1948, p. 1.
24. Rita Fitzpatrick, "Slayer, 13, Pleads Guilty," *Chicago Daily Tribune*, February 22, 1948, p. 1.
25. Rita Fitzpatrick, "Lang Weeps Over 22 Year Murder Term," *Chicago Daily Tribune*, April 21, 1948, p. 1.
26. "Killer of Boy Beats Witness Against Him," *Chicago Daily Tribune*, October 18, 1951, p. 1; "Killer Lang Gets Year for Slugging Boy," *Chicago Daily Tribune*, March 15, 1952, p. B7.
27. "Lang Boy Can't Explain Why He Slew Lonnie," *Chicago Daily Tribune*, April 3, 1948, p. 13.
28. "Low Mentality of Boy Slayer Cited in Appeal," *Chicago Daily Tribune*, March 6, 1948, p. 15.
29. "Court Refuses Plea of Lang Attorney to View 'Killer' Movie," *Chicago Daily Tribune*, March 26, 1948, p. 17.
30. Alice Myers, "Chicago Proposes Group to Control Crime Comics," *Christian Science Monitor*, September 14, 1948, p. 14.
31. "Educators Push Ban on 'Comic Books,'" *Christian Science Monitor*, April 29, 1948, p. 15.
32. "Chicago Sentiment Rises Against Juvenile 'Comics,'" *Christian Science Monitor*, June 8, 1948, p. 1.
33. Alice Meyer, "Action Speeds in Chicago to Curb Comics," *Christian Science Monitor*, October 6, 1948, p. 7.
34. "Question Boy, 9, in Slaying," *Chicago Daily Tribune*, May 28, 1948, p. 1.
35. "Sex Motive Admitted in Girl Killing," *Chicago Daily Tribune*, May 29, 1948, p. 1.
36. "Sex Slayer Insists Drowning of Boy, 6, in 1945 Accidental," *Chicago Daily Tribune*, June 2, 1948, p. 7; "Surly and Insolent, 14 Year Old Slayer Blocks Mental Tests," *Chicago Daily Tribune*, June 22, 1948, p. 5.
37. "Comic Book Fan, 14, Convicted of Murder," *Hartford Courant*, August 28, 1948, p. 13.
38. "Delinquency Traced to Four Potent Causes," *Christian Science Monitor*, March 20, 1947, p. 12.
39. Paul Lopes, *Demanding Respect: The Evolution of the American Comic Book* (Philadelphia: Temple University Press, 2009), pp. 30, 38.
40. "PTA Moves to Wipe Out Evil Comics," *Hartford Courant*, November 12, 1948, p. 5; "PTA Forms Action Committee to Eliminate Unfunny Comics," *Christian Science Monitor*, November 16, 1948, p. 13; "PTA Urges Study of Comic Books, Films, and Radio," *Chicago Daily Tribune*, September 17, 1948, p. A7; Bess Wilson, "PTA Moves to Curb Harmful Comic Books," *Los Angeles Times*, September 10, 1948, p. C1.
41. "Comic Books Held Harmful to Youth," *New York Times*, May 5, 1948, p. 35.
42. "Bishop Attacks Some Comic Books," *Baltimore Sun*, October 18, 1948, p. 28.
43. "Police Fight Comic Books," *New York Times*, August 12, 1947, p. 20.
44. "Police Blame Lurid Comics in Delinquency," *Christian Science Monitor*, July 31, 1947, p. 16.
45. "PTA Urges Study of Comic Books, Films, and Radio."
46. "Educators Push Ban on 'Comic Books,'" *Christian Science Monitor*, April 29, 1948, p. 15.
47. "700 Students See Hope for Comics," *New York Times*, January 5, 1949, p. 29.
48. "Pupils Burn Comic Books," *New York Times*, December 23, 1948, p. 22.
49. Lopes, p. 47.

50. Parent, "Banning the Comics," *Hartford Courant*, June 18, 1948, p. 18.
51. Onlooker, "Clean up the Comics," *Hartford Courant*, June 21, 1948, p. 8.
52. Morton F. Schweitzer, Letter to the Editor, "Comic Book Program," *Hartford Courant*, October 2, 1948, p. 8.
53. "Sociologist Scores Talk of Rising Delinquency," *Hartford Courant*, May 30, 1948, p. C7.
54. "Comics, As Evils, Called Overrated," *New York Times*, February 20, 1949, p. 31.
55. "Parents are Warned not to Blame Comic Books for Juvenile Crime," *New York Times*, October 7, 1948, p. 31.
56. "Roots of Delinquency," *Chicago Daily Tribune*, December 16, 1948, p. 22.
57. "Drive Planned to Eliminate Crime Comics," *Los Angeles Times*, June 30, 1948, p. A8.
58. "Detroit Prohibits Sale of 36 Comic Books," *Hartford Courant*, April 29, 1948, p. 1.
59. "Three Cities Curb Comics," *New York Times*, May 25, 1948, p. 25; "Agree on City Plan to Censor Comic Books," *Chicago Daily Tribune*, July 22, 1948, p. 15.
60. "So They Read Comics," *Hartford Courant*, July 5, 1948, p. 6.
61. "Crime and Comics," *Hartford Courant*, June 11, 1948, p. 14; "They Can Stand a Cleanup," *Hartford Courant*, June 22, 1948, p. 12.
62. "The Wrong Remedy," *Chicago Daily Tribune*, July 24, 1948, p. 6.
63. Bradford W. Wright, *Comic Book Nation: The Transformation of Youth Culture in America* (Baltimore: The Johns Hopkins University Press, 2001), p. 103.
64. "Clean-Up Started by Comics Books as Editors Adopt Self-Policing Plan," *New York Times*, July 2, 1948, p. 23.
65. Cynthia Lowry, "Comic Book Code Drawn," *Baltimore Sun*, August 29, 1948, p. 65.
66. "Cleaning up the Comics," *Hartford Courant*, July 8, 1948, p. 12.
67. Wright, pp. 103–104.
68. Hajdu, p. 150.
69. *Winters v. New York*, 333 US 507 (1948), http://supreme.justia.com/cases/federal/us/333/507.
70. Wright, p. 105.
71. "Comic Book Censorship," *New York Times*, February 25, 1949, p. 22.
72. Joseph Bruce Gorman, *Kefauver: A Political Biography* (New York: Oxford University Press, 1971), p. 197.
73. Ibid.
74. United Press, "Comics Held No Factor in Delinquency," *Washington Post*, November 12, 1950, p. M20.
75. "Crime and the Comics," *New York Times*, November 14, 1950, p. 30.
76. Peter Kihss, "Senator Charges 'Deceit' on Comics," *New York Times*, April 23, 1954, p. 29.
77. Hajdu, p. 201.
78. Senate transcripts, www.thecomicbooks.com/1954senatetranscripts.html.
79. Wright, p. 172.
80. Ibid., p. 174.
81. Senate transcripts, www.thecomicbooks.com/1955senateinterim.html.
82. Ibid.
83. "It's Wonderful!" *Christian Science Monitor*, September 18, 1954, p. 18.
84. "Kefauver Reports Comics Improved," *Christian Science Monitor*, March 29, 1956, p. 10.
85. Wright, pp. 92–93.
86. Ibid., pp. 94–95.
87. Kelcey Edwards, *Wonder Women! The Untold Story of American Superheroines*. Directed by Kristy Guevara-Flanagan, Vaquera Films, 2012, www.pbs.org/independentlens/wonder-women.
88. "Penologists Urged to Combat Comics," *Christian Science Monitor*, September 3, 1948, p. 2.

89. Ibid.
90. "Juvenile Delinquency Seen on Increase," *New York Times*, June 24, 1948, p. 22.
91. Senate transcripts, www.thecomicbooks.com/1955senateinterim.html.
92. C. Wright Mills, "Nothing to Laugh at," *New York Times*, April 25, 1954, p. BR20.
93. Robert S. Warshow, "The Study of Man: Paul, The Horror Comics, and Dr. Wertham," *Commentary*, June 1, 1954, www.commentarymagazine.com/article/the-study-of-man-paul-the-horror-comics-and-dr-wertham.
94. "Bad Comic Books are Very Bad," *Washington Post*, November 9, 1954, p. 33.
95. Hajdu, pp. 259, 233.
96. Tilley, p. 393.
97. Ibid., p. 394.
98. Ibid., pp. 396, 399.
99. Ibid., pp. 402, 404.
100. Beaty, p. 24.
101. Ibid., p. 67; Hajdu, p. 99.
102. Hajdu, p. 112.
103. James Gilbert, "Mass Culture and the Fear of Delinquency," *Journal of Early Adolescence*, 5 (1985), pp. 505–516.
104. National Center for Education Statistics, "Percentage of the Population Enrolled in School, by Age Group: Selected Years, 1940–2010," (Washington, DC: US Department of Education, 2011), http://nces.ed.gov/programs/digest/d11/tables/dt11_007.asp.
105. Gilbert, *A Cycle of Outrage*, p. 41.
106. Springhall, pp. 134, 127.
107. "Penologists Urged to Combat Comics," *Christian Science Monitor*, September 3, 1948, p. 2.
108. Federal Bureau of Investigation, *Crime in the United States, 1945* (Washington, DC: FBI, 1945), p. 94.
109. Federal Bureau of Investigation, *Crime in the United States*, various years (Washington, DC: FBI, 1944–1946).
110. Gilbert, "Mass Culture," pp. 505–516.
111. Hajdu, p. 85.
112. Gilbert, "Mass Culture," p. 513.
113. Daniels, p. 86.
114. Hajdu, pp. 330.
115. Wright, pp. 176, 152.
116. For more discussion see Marjorie Heins, *Not in Front of the Children: "Indecency," Censorship, and the Innocence of Youth* (New Brunswick, NJ: Rutgers University Press, 2007).
117. Hajdu, pp. 326, 329.
118. Daniels, pp. 83, 180.
119. Springhall, pp. 141–146.
120. About Comic-Con International, San Diego Comic Convention, accessed March 19, 2014, www.comic-con.org/about.
121. Glenn Elert (ed.), "Number of Televisions in the US," *The Physics Fact Book*, 2007, http://hypertextbook.com/facts/2007/TamaraTamazashvili.shtml.
122. Hajdu, p. 7.

5

ANTI-MUSIC CRUSADES

Fears of Racial Integration, Religious
Participation, and Freedom of Expression

In 1955, the *Los Angeles Times* described rock and roll as "a violent, harsh type of music, that, parents feel, incites teenagers to do all sorts of crazy things."[1] "Teenagers virtually work themselves into a frenzy," a police superintendent told the *Hartford Courant* that same year.[2] In an editorial a few months later, the *Courant* described teens as "rock and roll addicts," and "fanatics addicted to this latest craze," wearing "bizarre zoot suits," who are ultimately a "public nuisance and a threat to public safety."[3] According to critics, the music itself was dangerous; a prominent psychiatrist called rock and roll a "contagious disease."[4]

The mayor of Asbury Park, New Jersey, "blamed the music for 'trouble all around the country.'"[5] Two separate *Baltimore Sun* stories called rock and roll "turbulent" and claimed it "sparks teenage unrest and contributes to juvenile delinquency."[6] "Whenever there was teen-age trouble, we found rock and roll in the background," reported the Pennsylvania Chiefs of Police Association.[7] When a 1959 show hosted by Dick Clark was banned in Minneapolis "for the peace and well-being of the city," the police chief said that he was "certain violence will occur again."[8] A fight at a Newport, Rhode Island, naval base was described as "a riot touched off by rock 'n' roll rhythms."[9]

These concerns were not limited to the United States. A 1957 *New York Times* article claimed that rock and roll caused global pandemonium: "Youngsters have torn up theater seats in London . . . In Vancouver, BC, a singer had to be rescued by police when a crowd of 2,000 juveniles he was entertaining went wild." In Japan, the movie *Rock Around the Clock* supposedly caused a riot as well.[10] During Soviet control of Eastern Europe, Western music—particularly rock and roll—was banned as a threat to state authority. But its appeal remained strong; sales of songs carved into discarded x-ray films sold at a premium in underground markets. Music came to represent personal freedom to its secret listeners, and potential anarchy to totalitarian regimes.

In this chapter we will look at some of the many moral crusades against popular music during the twentieth century. Crusades against jazz, rock and roll, rap, and heavy metal could each fill a whole book. This chapter is by no means an exhaustive look at such crusades, but mostly considers the years between 1950 through the 1980s in order to better understand the context of the mid- to late twentieth century moral crusaders. These complaints about music serve as a backlash to the shift towards personal expression and away from conformity, drawing fire from religious leaders who saw anti-authority themes in music as particularly threatening.

It shouldn't be a surprise that when white audiences started listening to jazz and, later, to rock and roll and rap, this would trigger fears of racial integration in a highly segregated America, along with concerns about sexuality. And with growing fears of delinquency in the postwar era, the combination of rock and roll and integration would lead to fears of youth violence.

Many people have served as anti-music moral crusaders; this chapter focuses on their complaints and underlying interest, from a segregationist fighting against the civil rights movement, clergy members who feared that their influence over young people was waning, and politicians seeking to appeal to their constituents' concerns about the expansion of freedom of expression. Moral crusaders blamed music for a host of problems, including youth violence and teen pregnancy. Music lyrics did become more explicit over the course of the century, troubling parents and other adults. Musicians could easily serve as folk devils, especially those that toyed with dark imagery, sang sexually explicit lyrics, or seemed to derive the mass adoration that parents and religious leaders feared threatened their influence over children. Young fans of music, be it early rock and roll, rap, or other forms that moral crusaders railed against, were also easily stigmatized as potential dangers to themselves and others.

As with comic books and pinball, mid-century concerns about rock and roll coincided with heightened attention to juvenile delinquency. Anti-music crusades span much of the twentieth century and reflect concerns about social changes such as integration, fears of delinquency, and changes in involvement in traditional religious activities and freedom of expression that would ignite moral crusaders to do something about new forms of music. The economic growth of the postwar era led to the increasing purchasing power of young listeners, who were creating separate subcultures with their own unique soundtracks. As a marker of youth culture, which would be politicized in the later decades of the twentieth century, music seemed threatening to the old social order.

Fear, Music, and Race

Today, jazz aficionados are older and more educated than the rest of the population, but when jazz first became popular it was considered dangerous and "uncivilized." The opposite is true today; according to a National Endowment for the Arts (NEA) study, of those who attended jazz concerts, more than half had a college degree or higher and nearly half were part of the highest income groups ($75,000 a year or more); those with incomes of $150,000 a year or more were the most likely to report listening to jazz. Most fans are between 45 and 64 years of age, according to the report.[11] But in the past, the musical genre associated with African Americans led to racialized fears of jazz and jazz musicians. The idea that whites might even *admire* African American musicians furthered concerns about jazz's influence. As we will see, similar fears of rock and roll and rap reflected concerns about the shifting racial order later in the twentieth century. African American influence on popular music would grow throughout the century, challenging old racial hierarchies.

In 1933, Adolf Hitler banned jazz from the Berlin Broadcasting Station, "especially that brand produced by Negro orchestras and singers."[12] By 1935, "Negro jazz" was banned from all German radio on the grounds that it "has had a demoralizing effect," according to the radio director of the Third Reich, who also called jazz "the manifestation of the culture of a semi-wild people" which instead "belongs in a museum of racial history."[13]

Germany was not the only country where complaints about jazz took on explicit racial overtones. In the US, the birthplace of jazz, a New York high school student won a 1922 essay contest for claiming that "jazz has taken its hold on weak-minded people," blaming "jazz-like music" for making Austria "a country of maniacs." The winner concluded: "Jazz indicates a tendency toward insanity." The second prize winner called jazz "the call of the wild," which she likened to "the barbarians of Africa and the savage Indians of America." Civilization itself would "recede" thanks to jazz and other forms of popular music.[14]

Jazz allegedly caused all sorts of problems. "Jazz is Said to Cause America's Unrest," according to a 1926 letter to the editor of the *Baltimore Sun*, who claimed that the music was more dangerous than "light wines" during Prohibition. "All of the foundling sins of America for six years . . . sex immorality, lawlessness, rotten plays, the white slave traffic, drug traffic . . . it was jazz and the war that bent us so."[15]

The music "has much the same effect on young people and should be legislated against," a Kansas City school superintendent noted in 1922, calling jazz "debasing and degrading music."[16] Jazz purportedly led to "vulgar dancing," according to the *New York Tribune* in 1921, and called into question the legal definition of "proper dancing" in Long Beach, California, that same year.[17] When a Brooklyn musician jumped from his window and into a snow bank in 1926, the *New York Times* reported that he had "come under the spell of the music," which apparently caused him to "snap under the strain."[18] This same music called "beastly, sentimental, and vulgar" in the *New York Tribune* was also banned in Soviet Russia for being part of "bourgeois culture."[19]

Perhaps it shouldn't be a surprise that jazz would elicit concern. Musically it is a break from tradition, unrestrained, often improvised and free-flowing. It also was a distinctively African American influence on culture and, while not the first, one that coincided with the Jim Crow era and white anxieties about maintaining the racial order. Not coincidentally, moral crusades against music later in the twentieth century would focus primarily on genres such as rock and roll and rap, both initially created by African American musicians.

The rise of jazz in the early decades of the twentieth century parallels the rebirth of the Ku Klux Klan and the success of D. W. Griffith's *The Birth of a Nation*, which glorified the Klan as a chivalrous protector of white womanhood. Concerns about "white slavery," or white women supposedly forced into prostitution, rose at the turn of the century, leading to the passage of the Mann Act (also called the White Slave Traffic Act), which made transporting females across state lines for "immoral purposes" a federal offense.

In the early decades of the twentieth century, music genres clearly denoted and reinforced segregation. In the mid-1940s, *Billboard* magazine categorized African American jazz, blues, and gospel performers' songs as "race records"—this category later became "rhythm and blues." (At that time, an also unflattering "hillbilly record" category existed for what we know now as country music.)

As journalist Larry Birnbaum details, jazz, blues, and other forms of traditionally African American musical genres contributed to the creation of rock and roll. Duke Ellington called rock and roll "the most raucous form of jazz"; Birnbaum concludes that "the assimilation of African American music by whites is virtually the story of American popular music from the eighteenth century onward."[20]

"The words 'rock and roll' appeared in titles or lyrics of blues, jazz, and gospel songs throughout the 1920s and 1930s," Birnbaum notes; the phrase even appeared in religious songs in the nineteenth century.[21] The phrase sometimes connoted sex, but not always. "Rather than simply signifying sex, 'rock' and 'roll' were ambiguous terms, typical of slang in general and African American slang in particular," Birnbaum explains. "Sexual expression has always been more overt in

African American jazz, blues, and R&B than in mainstream white pop."[22]

The onset of World War II led to nearly full employment and helped spur a massive migration of African Americans from the South to the industrial North and Midwest. With a bit more prosperity, African Americans became a commercial target market, especially for radio programming when the introduction of television ended most radio programs. Rhythm and blues music would begin to draw young listeners of all backgrounds via the airwaves.[23]

Few agree on the precise beginning of the genre that came to be called rock and roll, but the music began to get the attention of white audiences starting around 1953, particularly when white disc jockey Alan Freed began playing the music on his Cleveland radio show.[24] The following year Elvis Presley's first single, "That's All Right," was released, and in 1955 the film *Blackboard Jungle*, about a tough inner-city school, featured the song "Rock Around the Clock" in its opening credits. That year a handful of news stories ran about the supposed dangers of rock and roll concerts; by 1956 there would be an onslaught of complaints, as rock and roll began to dominate commercial radio.[25]

Moral Crusaders, Race, and Rock and Roll

For segregationists, the growing popularity of rock and roll among whites in the early 1950s signaled their worst fears coming to fruition: young people were ignoring racial boundaries to enjoy the same music, and even accepting and admiring African American artists, or at least music derived from black performers. "So long as rhythm and blues music remained within the traditional boundaries defined by the pop music business, the opposition from white America was inconsequential," noted journalist John A. Jackson.[26] But once white teens took interest in the music, it became a problem. Many communities passed legislation banning interracial dancing.[27]

In Birmingham, Alabama, white supremacist activist Asa Carter suggested that rock and roll and music featuring African American artists be banned from jukeboxes.[28] Rock and roll and jazz contained "degenerate, animalistic beats and rhythms," he said in 1956. "This savage and primitive type of music which comes straight from Africa brings out the base things in man." He also claimed that the National Association for the Advancement of Colored People (NAACP) "uses this type of music as a means of pulling the white man down to the level of the Negro."[29] He saw rock and roll as a plot by the NAACP and those in favor of integration "for the purpose of undermining the morals of white people."[30]

Carter was essentially a professional race-baiter and provocateur, able to garner first local and then the national spotlight for his pro-segregation crusade. When schools in Clinton, Tennessee, were desegregated in 1956, Carter traveled there to lead rallies and gin up mobs, leading to riots. He founded the North Alabama White Citizen's Council after a falling out with the Alabama White Citizen's Council (AWCC) over Carter's anti-Semitic speeches (the AWCC wanted to focus primarily on preventing racial integration). He later went on to write speeches for George Wallace when he ran for governor of Alabama in 1962; Carter wrote the famous speech with the line "segregation now, segregation tomorrow, segregation forever."[31]

Music was not Carter's main focus, but as white youth began listening to African American musicians, he and other segregationists feared the artists' influence, particularly by playing on fears that white women would be vulnerable to black male performers' charms.

In one incident, his group picketed a Birmingham concert—ironically, a whites-only show featuring performers such as Bill Haley & His Comets—in their "campaign against . . . 'Negro Music.'" Protesters carried signs that read, "Jungle Music Promotes Integration" and "Be-Bop Promotes Communism."[32] Members of the group even attacked African American singer Nat King Cole as he performed in Birmingham, but were arrested by police at the event. The group was allegedly trying to incite other white men to attack Cole—although not a rock and roll performer—and had numerous weapons in a parked car, leading to speculation that they were interested in seriously harming him.[33]

The growing popularity of rock and roll was likely an opportunity to garner national media attention for Carter, whose cause was a much larger one than the music. The music provided evidence that the tide against segregation was clearly turning. But his ability to get attention and draw supporters indicated that racism was a significant factor in many critics' disdain for rock and roll.

Criticism with racial overtones did not just come from avowed white supremacists. In 1956, psychiatrist Francis J. Braceland—who would become president of the American Psychiatric Association—called rock and roll music a "communicable disease," and "cannibalistic and tribalistic."[34] Fellow psychiatrist Jules Masserman told the *Washington Post* that same year that rock and roll is "primitive quasi-music that can be traced back to prehistoric cultures." The *Post* described the music as: "a combination of many forms of music, from the most primitive jungle beats to the sensuous rhythms of Negro blues to the monotonous cacophony of hillbilly happiness numbers."[35] The *Baltimore Sun* described how fans "got close to jungle enthusiasm" at a local concert.[36] And the *Hartford Courant* claimed that "an entertainer known as Tutti-Fruitti [sic]" told the newspaper:

> Rock-and-roll music is derived from the tribal tom-tom beats of primitive savages. Their music form is the simplest known. Lacking imagination to create melody or the intricate rhythms of civilized music, the savages depended upon the highly repetitious rhythm of their drums to excite emotion for tribal dances . . . The listener's emotions, particularly the baser ones, are aroused.[37]

Just as with jazz before it, many critics of rock and roll referenced the supposed "savage" nature of the music, a thinly-veiled reference to its African American roots. Couched in these racialized fears were concerns about violence. The *Christian Science Monitor* explained that critics "maintain that the savage beat of the music incites some teenagers to misdeeds and acts of violence."[38] A reader in Pittsburgh wrote to a local newspaper that complaints about delinquency were not the main reason people were concerned about rock and roll. "The real reason is 'integration.' It is going along too smoothly for some evil minds and they have blamed it on rock 'n' roll music."[39]

Rock and Roll, Race, and Violence

News accounts highlighted the incidents of violence at rock concerts when they happened, be they small fistfights and arrests for use of foul language or larger alcohol-fueled skirmishes. If the audience stood up, danced, screamed, and refused to sit and listen to the music quietly the press might have said that a "riot" took place. Police intervention, and in some cases provocation, likely played a role in the many skirmishes reported in the press.[40]

Many headlines gave the impression that rock and roll shows were sites of danger, suggesting riots regularly broke out at concerts. For instance "Rock and Riot" (*Hartford Courant*, 1955), "Teenagers Riot at Rock 'n' Roll in Mt. Vernon" (*New York Amsterdam News*, 1957), "Indictment to be Sought in 'Rock' Riot" (*Washington Post*, 1958), and "Teen-Agers Turn Show into Rock, Roll Riot" (*Hartford Courant*, 1959) all suggested that the concerts and the teens who attended needed to be stopped. A 1958 story describes "mobs of hoodlums . . . menacing adults in wolf-pack fashion," echoing claims that rock and roll created awakened primitive, animalistic tendencies in its listeners.[41]

Authorities in several cities took action, banning rock concerts altogether. Bridgeport, Connecticut, Asbury Park, New Jersey, Santa Cruz, California, Newport, Rhode Island, New Haven, Connecticut, Birmingham, Alabama, Minneapolis, Minnesota, and Boston, Massachusetts at one time banned rock and roll acts from performing during the 1950s, citing public safety concerns.

These stories were especially likely to report that interracial violence (or violence against whites) took place at or immediately after a concert, seeming to support moral crusader Asa Carter's fear of the dangers of rock and roll and interracial audiences. If the beat of the music caused young people to become violent—especially if white teens were the victims—controlling and restricting the music seemed justified. When two Connecticut teens were injured after a concert, the *Hartford Courant* described the event as "a minor riot." According to the newspaper's account, "they and three other Waterbury teenagers were set upon by 15 or 20 young Negroes," which, the story noted, "started when remarks were passed"—about what, we don't know, nor do we know exactly who started the fight.[42] In 1957, the *New York Times* reported that "Knife fights and gunfire erupted from a mass of interracial rock 'n roll fans outside an auditorium" in Dallas, leaving six wounded, allegedly "by a Negro after an argument."[43]

That same year the *Times* reported that in Boston, "A 15-year-old white boy was stabbed and thrown onto the tracks at a subway station . . . during a fight between white and Negro boys and girls following a rock 'n roll show." The concert "feature[d] a majority of Negro performers," and a police lieutenant claimed that "the Negro youths were responsible for it" in a story called "Rock 'n' Roll Fight Hospitalizes Youth."[44] The lieutenant said the victim was "a nice kid, minding his own business," implying that unsuspecting white youth attending rock shows were at risk of becoming victims of random African American violence.[45]

At a Newport, Rhode Island, naval base in 1956, enlisted men listening to Fats Domino participated in a "beer-bottle throwing, chair-swinging riot," according to a *New York Times* report. According to the commanding officer, "the only cause of the melee among white and Negro sailors and marines . . . was the excitement accompanying the fever-pitched 'Rock 'n' Roll.'" The officer went on to ban rock and roll shows from the base for at least a month.[46]

These and other stories suggest that rock concerts were cites of racial violence, particularly racial violence against white youth. During the height of the civil rights movement, these stories would be especially incendiary. Stories of racial violence against African Americans were seldom reported on in the mainstream press, but did appear in the black press. The *Los Angeles Sentinel*, for instance, reported in 1960 that "three Negroes were shot . . . during an altercation during a Sunday 'rock and roll' show" in Birmingham, Alabama.[47]

After a fight broke out during a 1957 show at the Boston Garden, five teens were charged with "disturbing a public assembly" leading a judge to suggest that no more permits be granted to rock and roll shows. "Things got out of kilter when the beat got to rocking," a *Pittsburgh Courier* story about the incident notes. (A 40-year-old woman was also arrested at the concert.)[48]

When violence broke out at famed disk jockey Alan Freed's "The Big Beat" concert featuring a variety of artists in May 1958, five cities banned the show. At the Boston event, reports suggested that 15 people "were stabbed, beaten, and robbed by gangs of teen-agers," although no arrests were made.[49] Some accounts cast doubt that any violence took place inside the arena at all; the location of the Boston Arena was considered a rough part of town where street robberies were common.[50] According to a witness, the incident was "simply another case of enthusiastic teenagers dancing in the aisles, standing on seats, and crowding the stage."[51] When police threatened to turn on the house lights if the audience members didn't sit down, Freed apparently encouraged the audience to sit down. They did, but once the next act took the stage they got up again.

After authorities turned on the house lights, apparently to stop fans from dancing in the aisles, Freed allegedly apologized, saying "It looks like the police in Boston don't want you kids to have any fun."[52] According to Freed's biographer, the DJ "hated Boston" due to what he saw as heavy-handed police tactics; a police officer allegedly told Freed "we don't like your kind of music here." The district attorney blamed "rock and roll paganism" for encouraging juvenile delinquency.[53]

Days later Freed was indicted for "incit[ing] the unlawful destruction of real and personal property," for which he could have served three years in jail or a $1,000 fine.[54] The charges were later dropped, and Freed claimed he was a scapegoat, as was rock and roll.[55]

Rock and roll was becoming a big business, and some promoters were clearly in over their heads, admitting too many people to shows with too little attention paid to crowd control as events drew large numbers, including people who had been drinking. If fights broke out, the limited presence of security or the amount of alcohol consumption seldom drew as much attention as the type of music and its youthful fans.

If these complaints sound familiar, they should. While it might seem tempting to think that the racialized fears of the 1950s were put to rest following the gains of the civil rights movement, stories about violence at rap concerts also mark spaces where young African Americans gather as sources of concern.

Just as 1950s headlines warned that rock and roll shows were dangerous, news in the 1980s and 1990s focused on the alleged danger of rap concerts. The headlines were similar to those from the 1950s: "Eighteen are Arrested After Rap Concert" (*New York Times*, 1986), "One Killed, Five Injured and Sixteen Arrested at Rap Concert" (*New York Times*, 1987), "Teens Trampled After Rap Concert" (*Washington Post*, 1987), and "Nine Charged, Four With Murder, in Robbery Spree at LI Rap Concert" (*New York Times*, 1988). Stories reported on violence at rap concerts so regularly that when none occurred at a 1992 Madison Square Garden concert, the *New York Times* reported on it as though it were an anomaly.[56]

While it may seem self-evident from these headlines that rap concerts provoked violence, even murder, and were thus more dangerous than the rock and roll "riots" of the 1950s, many of the incidents happened after or outside of the actual venues. Nationwide, violent crime had been on the rise in the late 1980s, not just in concert halls. And, just like in the 1950s, concertgoers challenged that reports of violence were overblown.[57] Violence at concerts was certainly not limited to rap shows; just as in the 1950s, criminals found opportunities late at night after shows end outside of concert venues, as was the case after a 1986 Run-DMC concert ended at Madison Square Garden in New York.[58]

When reporting on concert violence, news stories commonly invoked a list of other incidents, much as they did in the 1950s with rock and roll shows. After a fatal stabbing at a 1988 concert, the *St. Petersburg Times* reported that it "was the latest in a series of violent incidents at rap concerts around the nation."[59]

Using much the same rationale and language as concert promoters did in the 1950s, rap concerts became categorically defined as sites of trouble. In 1986, the *Washington Post* reported that "several hundred street gang members rushed the front row and had what appeared . . . to be a prearranged turf fight" at a Run-DMC concert in Long Beach, California. Following this, the venue refused to "book or allow to take place any attraction whose patrons have caused or who have a propensity to create situations likely to cause injury to any other patrons," according to the *Post*. Many other venues refused to book rap acts, echoing bans of the early rock and roll era.

The *Washington Post* reported that by 1989, "concerns about concert violence" meant that "tours are having an increasingly hard time finding hospitable venues across the country." Darryll Brooks of the group G Street told the *Post* that when "the stars and the audience are young and black" fears of concert violence rise.[60] When a 1991 Washington, DC, concert was oversold and ticketholders were turned away, police arrived to disperse the crowd of several hundred angry ticketholders. A witness told the *Washington Post* that he thought the police had overreacted: "They see a bunch of black youths and they believe there will be violence."[61]

While during the civil rights era resistance to integration created more overtly racist critiques of early rock and roll, by the 1980s the racialized language was more covert. But race was still at the center of fears about rap music in the 1980s and 1990s. Instead of blatant racial slurs, the use of terms like "gang infested," used to describe a concert in Detroit, invokes the same meanings as "tribal" and "primitive" did 30 years prior.[62] "Roaming teens" in the 1950s became the 1980s "roaming gangs," apparently wreaking havoc at concerts.[63] Highlighting suspects' neighborhoods also implicitly alludes to their race, as American cities remained geographically segregated decades after legal desegregation.

Just as with early rhythm and blues and rock and roll, rap didn't get much negative attention until white teens began listening and buying records in the mid-1980s. As sociologist Amy Binder notes, rap received much more criticism than genres such as rock or heavy metal because rap was framed by news accounts and detractors as a danger to society, not just to individual listeners.[64] As an art form that communicated feelings of disempowerment in largely segregated urban centers, rap lyrics regularly expressed anger towards deeply entrenched inequality and police brutality. For instance, Ice-T's song, "Cop Killer," received national attention and protests followed his performances.

Critics argued that violent lyrics promoted violence, while ignoring the broader contexts in which the song was written.[65]

As music critic Jon Pereles wrote in the *New York Times* in 1992:

> When suburbia embraced hip-hop during the 1980s, the alarmist reactions only increased . . . In the mainstream American imagination, blacks have historically been considered the Other, the opposite of the mainstream's genteel self-image. That mysterious, imagined Other is considered uncivilized, sex-crazed, irrational, angry.
>
> Hip-hop, many commentators have inveighed, is intended solely to spur violence, race hatred, and general lawlessness. Not so coincidentally, that's what those commentators fear from an urban black population whose prospects deteriorated steadily during the 1980s.[66]

Africana studies professor Tricia Rose writes that it is rap's resistance to oppression itself that led to its unique demonization, beyond that of predominantly white rock acts:

> Large arenas and other hostile social institutions that treat young African Americans with suspicion and fear are themselves often the subject of rappers' lyrics . . . The public school system, the police, and the popular media perceive and construct them as a dangerous internal element within urban America—an element that if allowed to roam freely will threaten the social order, an element that must be policed . . . It is this ideological position regarding Black youth that frames media and institutional attacks on rap and separates resistance to rap from attacks sustained by rock and roll artists.[67]

Complaints about jazz, early rock and roll, and rap are about more than just musical preference. These African American-influenced genres touched off concerns about the shifting status of African Americans in the United States, first about integration and later a reaction to black anger towards continued segregation and police aggression.

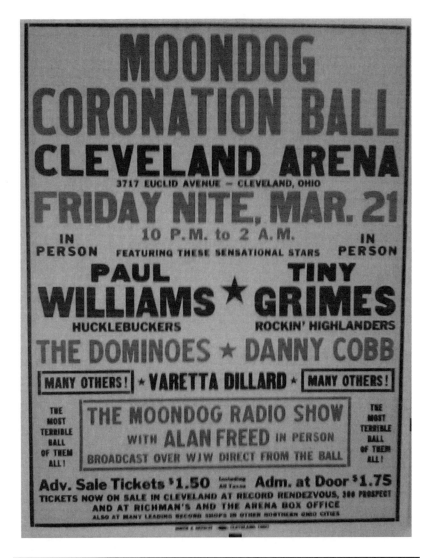

Figure 5.1 Cleveland disc jockey Alan Freed organized what is thought to be the first rock and roll concert, the Moondog Coronation Ball, in March 1952. It was shut down due to fears of rioting after the event drew more than twice the arena's capacity

Moral Crusaders, Music, and Religion

Changes in the racial order were not the only concerns of anti-music moral crusaders. For some, music idolatry became troubling: observers noted how many fans entered into an almost frenzied state in the presence of performers. At a time of change, with young people spending less time in the labor force and more time in school, and integration challenging the racial order of prior generations, some religious leaders wondered if musicians were becoming false idols and replacing traditional worship.

The affluence of the postwar era and the growing focus on materialism created what religious scholar Robert S. Ellsworth calls a "spiritual paradox" between conformity and freedom.[68] The freedom of self-expression in an age marked by the growth of mass media would challenge notions of conformity. Religious scholar Jason C. Bivins explains that critics of rock and roll sought to "promote moral codes that reinscribe conservative norms regarding race, gender, and sexuality and construct interpretive frames that posit certain kinds of social change and pluralism as threats."[69]

The rise of the Beatles in 1964 seemed to confirm the fear that teen idols were being worshipped, as thousands of shrieking teen girls appeared at their every arrival, at times challenging authority and violating expectations of mid-century femininity. "Beatlemania" drew massive crowds of people that sometimes fainted, overcome with emotion. Their reaction even surprised and drew concern from the Beatles themselves, who eventually tired of the chaos their personal appearances caused and quit touring altogether.

Reverend David Noebel found the band disturbing enough to publish *Communism, Hypnotism and the Beatles: An Analysis of the Communist Use of Music* in 1965, claiming that the Beatles were creating mental illness in young people, weakening America's future by colonizing the minds of its young. Noebel would certainly not be the last religious leader to find fault with the Beatles, and rock music more generally.

In 1966, two years after the group became popular in the US, John Lennon spoke to a reporter from the *London Evening Standard*, who noted that he "is reading extensively about religion." The article begins by describing some of the more mundane aspects of Lennon's daily life; nearly at the midpoint, reporter Maureen Cleave notes:

> Experience has sown few seeds of doubt in him: not that his mind is closed, but it's closed round whatever he believes at the

time. "Christianity will go," [Lennon] said. "It will vanish and shrink. I needn't argue about that; I'm right and I will be proved right. We're more popular than Jesus now; I don't know which will go first—rock 'n' roll or Christianity. Jesus was all right but his disciples were thick and ordinary. It's them twisting it that ruins it for me."[70]

This quote drew no reaction when it first appeared in the British news-paper in March 1966; religious leaders had often lamented the decline in the popularity of the Church of England. But when this quote was excerpted into *Datebook*, an American teen fan magazine that summer, just before the Beatles' US tour, a firestorm erupted.

Most who reacted likely only heard that Lennon said that the Beatles were "more popular than Jesus," which he did, but missed the context; he also said that rock and roll will also fade away. Rather than a young man boasting of his success and claiming to be more *important* than Jesus, as was often interpreted, Lennon appeared to be supportive of Jesus' teachings but critical of those who "twist it." Cleave attempted to clarify the context of Lennon's remarks, explaining that "he was deplor-ing rather than approving" that "to many people" the Beatles might be "better known than Jesus [. . .] He said that things had reached a ridiculous state of affairs when human beings could be worshiped in this extraordinary way."[71] This comment might have reflected Lennon's growing disenchantment with fame itself, and the crowds that followed the band.

Many radio stations in the South refused to play Beatles records; some radio stations in South Africa also banned their music.[72] Calls for record burnings, including one held by the Ku Klux Klan, took place that summer.[73] A minister in Cleveland threatened to "revoke the mem-bership of any members of [his] church that agree with John Lennon's remark about Jesus or go to see the Beatles."[74]

Some American clergy agreed with Lennon. A Presbyterian min-ister in Madison, Wisconsin, said that "there is much validity in what Lennon said. To many people, the golf course is also more popular than Jesus Christ."[75] A Phoenix radio station's musical director observed:

"We have placed more emphasis on material and physical things than religion. Religion in itself is good and wholesome but it's our fault that it's on its way out."[76]

This is precisely what many religious leaders feared. The frenzy over Lennon's remark likely touched on the belief that Americans were becoming less religious in the postwar era. Ironically, the years coinciding with the popularization of rock and roll were also those with the highest levels of religious service attendance in US history, with polls suggesting that 47 percent attended weekly in 1955 and 1958. In the 1960s, attendance dropped to 40 percent. (In a June 2010 Gallup poll, attendance was 43 percent.[77]) As Ellsworth writes, "people tend to go to church in their prime child-bearing years." So perhaps it is no surprise that as baby boomers grew into teens and young adults their families' religious attendance declined.[78]

Several young religious leaders began preaching the evils of rock and roll during the 1970s and 1980s, creating elaborate presentations that they took on the road and television talk shows. In large part a backlash to the cultural changes of the 1960s—with challenges to sexual mores and traditional notions of gender—these activists saw rock music and its performers as directly promoting sin to young people.

In 1967, former musician and disc jockey Bob Larson published *Rock & Roll: The Devil's Diversion*, and began to speak around the country about the alleged dangers of music. In addition to speaking about rock and roll, his other talks included "Drugs, Defilement and Death," "Astrology and the Age of Aquarius," as well as "Firewalking and Satanic Miracles."[79] In 1972 he told the *Hartford Courant* that rock and roll "propagandize[d] certain lifestyles." He found concerts particularly problematic. "For 90 minutes, these kids are like zombies. It is a mass indulgence orgy."[80] Evangelist Gary Greenwald preached of music causing violence, immorality, and drug use at an Anaheim, California, high school. "Luke-warm Christians have been steered from their commitments to Christ by rock music," the school's principal told the *Los Angeles Times* after a ceremonial album-smashing event.[81]

For some religious leaders, the popularity of rock music seemed to be in direct opposition to a Christian lifestyle and was thus considered satanic. "We're just trying to teach our young people that you don't have to be caught up in this satanic force of rock music in order to be popular," a Shelby, North Carolina, pastor said in 1976 before a record burning in their church parking lot. "Anything in a Christian life other than Christ Himself being a dominant force we feel is not right. If you're committed to rock 'n' roll, you can't be committed to God."[82]

Brothers Dan, Steve, and Jim Peters, all ministers from St. Paul, Minnesota, called rock music "the greatest satanic force in the world" in 1980. Hosting record burnings around the country, they reasoned:

> Knowing many of these rock stars are homosexual, bisexual, perverted, and involved in drugs, the occult, witchcraft, and satanic worship, and that the lyrics in many of their songs are suggestive, lewd, and even sacrilegious, we burn these items in obedience to Jesus Christ.[83]

One such record burning torched the music of the Eagles, Electric Light Orchestra (ELO), Shaun Cassidy, John Denver, the Bee Gees, Helen Reddy, and other 1970s pop music hit-makers.[84] When rain prevented one record burning, attendees ripped items thought "influenced by the devil," including Star Wars figurines. "Satan has pulled the wool over our eyes and brought things in that we didn't even realize," a participant noted.[85]

"The vast majority of rock music is out to destroy Christianity by destroying Christian morals," Al Menconi, a former teacher turned anti-rock crusader, told an audience during a 1984 presentation. "The Bible says musicians will lead the world in sorcery," he warned in his presentation, titled "Everything You Want to Know About Rock Music (Secular and Christian)."[86]

With the coming of age of baby boomers in the 1970s, the spiritual marketplace expanded as many people sought alternatives to mainstream religion. From self-help books and seminars to new religious sects and the growing influence of Eastern religions in the West, the search for guidance beyond traditional religious traditions created worry. Fears of cults, brainwashing, and satanic worship grew, particularly after the

1978 "Jonestown" tragedy in Guyana, where 909 people died in a mass murder/suicide.

Menconi considered a George Harrison album cover satanic because it contained "a Hindu symbol" and "subliminally glorified" the religion. Any music not considered Christian music was a waste of time, he told a group of students in 1981.[87] Menconi and several of his fellow anti-rock crusaders are still active in preaching the dangers of popular culture (Bob Larson has focused more recently on performing exorcisms). Perhaps in reaction to their critics, some forms of heavy metal used increasingly dark imagery such as inverted crosses, included brimstone-like fire in their concerts, and took on names like Black Sabbath.

For these moral crusaders, rock music represented the most visible driver of change during a period of significant social and cultural upheaval. Many young people challenged the war in Vietnam, the traditional racial order, traditional beliefs about sexuality and gender, and embraced physical pleasure—through sex and drugs—leading to a backlash against these shifts by those hoping to re-establish traditional mores. While many of these crusades came from conservative activists, their concerns would grow more mainstream when political leaders adopted many of their positions on cultural issues in the 1980s.

The Politics of Anti-Music Crusades

In the spring of 1982, California State Assembly's Consumer Protection and Toxic Materials Committee listened to Led Zeppelin's "Stairway to Heaven." Following allegations that when played backwards the song contained satanic messages, committee member Phillip Wyman proposed Assembly Bill 3741 that would mandate warning labels be placed on albums with "subliminal messages recorded backwards" for the purpose of increasing sales. He claimed that recording artists purposely put these messages on records, which "can manipulate our behavior without our knowledge and consent and turn us into disciples of the anti-Christ."[88]

The committee also heard the Beatles' "Revolution" and other songs played backwards, supposedly with messages praising Satan. Wyman claimed that listeners could unconsciously understand the message and then perhaps act upon it. A key witness, William H. Yarroll II, the president of a management consulting firm (whose claims of being a neuroscientist are unclear), said that many musicians are members of the "Church of Satan" and put the messages on as part of a "pact."[89] Apparently, one of Wyman's constituents saw Yarroll on a PTL ("Praise the Lord") network talk show earlier that year about backwards masking and contacted Wyman with her concerns.[90]

"Backwards masking doesn't exist," said a Warner Bros. representative, who was joined by other industry executives who flatly denied that musicians put backwards satanic messages in their songs. Scientists also debunked the idea that people would unconsciously follow subliminal messages. Psychologist Donald Lewis told the *Los Angeles Times* that research has shown "no effect. There is no evidence that subliminal messages can lead to behavioral change," particularly if these messages are backwards.[91]

And yet that summer, Representative Robert K. Dornan, also of California, proposed a similar bill in Congress, which would require a warning label stating "demonic messages when played backwards" on albums allegedly containing such messages. Congress declined to act on Dornan's "Demonic Messages Bill," just as the California State Assembly passed on Wyman's.[92]

If you've never heard a song on a vinyl record played backwards, it does sound disturbing. In the cultural context of the time, with concerns about religious decline coupled with numerous movies about satanic possession—*The Exorcist* (1973), *The Omen* (1976), and *The Amityville Horror* (1979) to name a few—Wyman and Dornan's claims would certainly get media attention. But not enough of their colleagues, or the public, bought the notion that musicians were in league with the devil and *purposely* planted these messages to convert an unsuspecting audience. But the audible lyrics—played forward, not backward—would get lawmakers' attention.

In 1984, the Parent Teacher Association (PTA) passed a resolution calling for a rating system for music, much like the one we have for movies. The next year "a group of Washington mothers"—who just happened to be married to a senator, the secretary of the Treasury, a former member of

Congress, and a former city council member—sent an open letter to the press to form a "grassroots movement" to try and pressure the music industry to clean up lyrics. They singled out Prince's sexually charged lyrics as particularly offensive; apparently a child of Tipper and Senator Al Gore had his album, *1999*, and they were shocked by lyrics about masturbation.[93]

The letter claims that "rock music has become increasingly pornographic." Drawing on earlier fears from religious leaders, the letter also claims that "some rock groups advocate satanic rituals . . . [and] of killing babies" and suggests that music also contributes to the "drug culture and what's happening today to our children."[94]

Not surprisingly, their letter got a tremendous amount of media attention, from the *Washington Post*, *Newsweek*, and *People* magazines, as well as national news networks. Within months of the letter a Senate hearing would be held, and the music in question would "stand trial," with testimony from musicians and critics alike.

The "Washington Wives," as they were called in the press, formed the Parents Music Resource Center (PMRC) in 1985 and, along with the PTA, called for a rating system, warning labels, and industry restraint. To make their case, the group highlighted what they called the "Filthy Fifteen," a list of 15 songs they found most disturbing based mostly on sexual content, but also including violence, drug and alcohol references, and the occult.

During the highly publicized hearings, Senator Ernest Hollings, Democrat from South Carolina, said that "the music in question does not have any redeeming social value. It's outrageous filth, and we've got to do something about it. If I could find some way to do away with it constitutionally, I would." PMRC co-founder Susan Baker, wife of Treasury Secretary James Baker, testified that "teen-age pregnancy and teen-age suicide rates are at epidemic proportions . . . and rape is up," suggesting that music was at least in part to blame for these problems.[95]

Actually, teen birth rates had *fallen* significantly since the mid-1950s, from more than 90 births per 1,000 to about 50 per 1,000 in the mid-1980s for 15- to 19-year-olds.[96] Rates of rape had *declined* by about half between 1975 and 1985, according to the National Crime Victimization Survey.[97] And while suicide rates for this age group did increase between 1970 and 1980, the rate for older people remained higher; in 1980, the median age of a suicide victim was about 40.[98]

Regardless of the actual statistics, there was a pervasive sense in the 1980s that young people needed reining in. The mainstreaming of complaints about music debasing the values of the nation's youth was a reaction to the sense of disorder felt after baby boomers came of age in the 1960s and 1970s. As the conservative movement gained political power, the idea that culture and values needed to change moved from the fringes to the political center in Washington, embraced by politicians of both parties.

Publically funded social programs would lose funding in favor of pushes for cultural changes, including warning labels on albums. In November 1985 the recording industry agreed to include a warning label that read "Parental Advisory—Explicit Lyrics" on some records.[99] The PMRC seemed to have won.

While the PMRC hoped the stickers were meant to be a badge of shame encouraging artists to clean up their lyrics, that clearly did not happen. A rash of songs specifically criticized—some rather colorfully— Tipper Gore and the PMRC.[100] Songs with explicitly sexual and violent lyrics likely *increased* in the 1990s. If anything, the warning labels heightened the "street cred" of up-and-coming artists, particularly with the growing popularity of so-called gangsta rap.

The Decline of the Anti-Music Crusades

The music industry feared that large retailers would not carry albums with warning stickers, which giant retailer Walmart would not. Some artists provided edited versions of music for sale there and to get radio airplay.[101] But music sales would change dramatically with the advent of digital MP3 files, easily shared after the introduction of the internet. No longer would consumers need to go to a brick and mortar store to buy music; in fact, the industry's biggest challenge was the new portability of music.

Even one of the "Washington Wives" changed her mind about the PMRC. When her husband first ran for president in 1987, Gore declared the hearings "a mistake" that "sent the wrong message," particularly as they began fundraising in New York and California to entertainment industry crowds.[102] In 1992, when Al Gore ran for vice-president, the PMRC was a faint memory for many, which helped him and running mate Bill Clinton attract young voters—many of them music-listening teens during the PMRC's heyday. Virtually no one remembered the PMRC when Gore was the Democratic Party's candidate for president in 2000.

The PMRC, religious leaders, and the music industry alike could not have predicted the ease through which music and other forms of popular culture could be shared in the 2010s with the ubiquity of smartphones and social networking technology. While the industry fights a sales slump and struggles to keep up with technological changes, it has never been easier for people to acquire, share, and enjoy music privately.

In 2005, more music was sold digitally than physically for the first time, and the gap continues to grow.[103] Vinyl has made a comeback of sorts for music aficionados and collectors, but it's now practically impossible to control the kinds of music young people listen to. Technology has also threatened the very existence of record labels, as artists can create and distribute their own music online now.

Learning from the Anti-Music Crusades

The notion of thousands of teens gathered to hear music that "seems to stir kids up," according to one public official, threatened more than the public order in and around a concert hall.[104] As the meaning of adolescence shifted, increasing towards a time of leisure in the postwar era, a new genre of music came to symbolize a break from the past. Rock and roll was "music for teenagers, about teenagers, performed by teenagers" at a time when teens seemed to be creating a separate subculture, according to historian Glenn C. Altschuler.[105] Authority figures, including parents and clergy, feared that this subculture would disregard traditional values as the social order was changing.

Anti-music moral crusaders came from diverse backgrounds, from segregationists to pastors to politicians and wives of political scions, but they all have one thing in common: a struggle to preserve what they see as slipping away. This might mean racial hierarchies, a more sanitized popular culture, or the power of religious leaders. In their campaigns against music, each sought to preserve the power and privilege of their authority: as white men, as adults, and moral leaders.

In constructing various genres of music as a public threat, moral crusaders also serve to cast musicians and fans as potentially threatening. Descriptions of teens as "rock and roll rioters" or the potential antichrist construct young people as folk devils, both vulnerable to the influence of music and dangerous to society at the same time. Condemning a genre of music is also a shortcut for constructing young people—often young people of color—as universally threatening, as we have seen with characterizations of rap. Music thus becomes a key way we construct meanings of deviance, by labeling listeners of a feared genre as a threat.

This ease of creating and sharing music, and any information really, has created a whole new set of fears. As we will see in the next chapter, popular culture is no longer only shared through mass media, but through micro media. We have our own audiences through social media, and it is far harder to control and monitor this content than ever before, creating new fears—and new ways of sharing those fears with others.

Notes

1. "Rock 'n' Roll Stage Show Frantic, Noisy," *Los Angeles Times*, November 4, 1955, p. B9.
2. "Bridgeport Police Ban Rock and Roll Dances," *Hartford Courant*, March 24, 1955, p. 23C.
3. "Rock and Riot," *Hartford Courant*, November 3, 1955, p. 18.
4. "Rock 'n' Roll Stage Show Frantic, Noisy."
5. "Resort Puts Freeze on Hot Music," *Hartford Courant*, July 12, 1956, p. 10A.
6. "Rock 'n' Roll Passes Test as Cool Eyes Watch Concert," *Baltimore Sun*, July 12, 1956, p. 36; "Police Stone-Cold to Rock 'n' Roll," *Baltimore Sun*, July 23, 1956, p. 3.
7. "Police Stone-Cold."
8. "Rock 'n' Roll Show is Banned in Minneapolis," *Hartford Courant*, October 20, 1959, p. 12A.
9. "'Rock 'n' Roll' Banned," *New York Times*, September 20, 1956, p. 29.
10. "Rock 'n' Roll Exported to 4 Corners of Globe," *New York Times*, February 23, 1957, p. 12.
11. National Endowment of the Arts, "2008 Survey of Public Participation in the Arts: Research Report #49" (Washington, DC: National Endowment of the Arts, 2009), p. 80, www.hennepintheatretrust.org/sites/default/files/NEA%20FULL%20Survey.pdf.
12. "American Jazz Banned From Radio by Hitler," *Washington Post*, March 6, 1933, p. 3.
13. "Jazz Banned on Air in Reich as Harmful to German Culture," *Baltimore Sun*, October 13, 1935, p. 1.
14. "Jazz vs. Classical Music," *Billboard*, June 10, 1922, p. 8.

15. Hayward Kendall, "Not Jugs but Jazz is Said to Cause America's Unrest," Letter to the Editor, *Baltimore Sun*, April 29, 1926, p. 12.

16. "Would Stop Jazz by Law," *Baltimore Sun*, February 12, 1922, p. 1

17. "Music is Pure, but Misused, Composer Tells Jazz Critics," *New York Tribune*, March 1, 1921, p. 20; "Blow Dust off Antijazz Law," *Los Angeles Times*, December 10, 1921, p. II 14.

18. "Jazz Music Blamed for Mad Flight," *New York Times*, February 19, 1926, p. 2.

19. "The War Upon Jazz," *New York Tribune*, March 5, 1921, p. 10; "Jazz Banned on Air."

20. Larry Birnbaum, *Before Elvis: The Prehistory of Rock 'n' Roll* (Lanham, MD: Scarecrow Press), 2013, p. 23.

21. Ibid., p. 19.

22. Ibid., p. 21.

23. Linda Martin and Kerry Segrave, *Anti-Rock: The Opposition to Rock 'n' Roll* (New York: Da Capo Press, 1993), p. 4.

24. Glenn C. Altschuler, *All Shook Up: How Rock 'n' Roll Changed America* (New York: Oxford University Press, 2003), pp. 20–21.

25. Ibid., p. 34.

26. John A. Jackson, *Big Beat Heat: Alan Freed and the Early Years of Rock and Roll* (New York: Schirmer Books, 1991), p. 72.

27. Altschuler, p. 40.

28. "'Rock 'n' Roll' Dilemma," *Los Angeles Sentinel*, April 12, 1956, p. A9.

29. Rob Roy, "Bias Against 'Rock 'n' Roll' Latest Bombshell in Dixie," *Daily Defender*, April 2, 1956, p. 19.

30. "'Rock and Roll' Labelled [sic] Weapon of Integration," *Atlanta Daily World*, March 30, 1956, p. 1.

31. See *The Reconstruction of Asa Carter*, Documentary, 2012, ITVS and Square Two Entertainment. Carter would go on to run for governor of Alabama in 1970, after feeling disappointed by what he saw as Wallace's capitulation on segregation. After his bid failed, he became a novelist under the pen name Forrest Carter, writing *The Rebel Outlaw: Josey Wales*, which Clint Eastwood went on to star in the film version of, and the bestselling *The Education of Little Tree*, which he claimed was a memoir about growing up part Cherokee, later found to also be a work of fiction.

32. "Alabama Pickets Rock-Roll Troupe," *Daily Defender*, May 21, 1956, p. 10.

33. D. L. Chandler, "Nat King Cole Attacked on Stage by White Supremacists in 1956," NewsOne, April 11, 2013, http://newsone.com/2373293/nat-king-cole-attacked-on-stage; Altschuler, p. 39.

34. Marion Jackson, "Ork Leaders Defend Rock & Roll Music," *Atlanta Daily World*, April 12, 1956, p. 7.

35. Phyllis Battle, "Rock 'n' Roll Music is Tops with Teen-Agers," *Washington Post*, June 24, 1956, p. F1.

36. "Rock 'n' Roll Passes Test as Cool Eyes Watch Concert," *Baltimore Sun*, July 12, 1956, p. 36.

37. Richard L. Mourey, "Experts Can't Explain Music," *Hartford Courant*, March 27, 1956, p. 1A. There is no clear evidence of who actually provided this opinion; Little Richard, who made the song "Tutti Frutti" popular in 1955, was not likely the source.

38. James Nelson Goodsell, "Rock 'n' Roll Opposition Rises," *Christian Science Monitor*, May 8, 1958, p. 3.

39. Al Woods, "Integration Cause of Rock, Roll Row," *Pittsburgh Courier*, Letter to the Editor, August 4, 1956, p. 11.

40. For more discussion, see Martin and Segrave, pp. 8, 33.

41. "Delinquency and Public Safety," *Daily Defender*, October 10, 1956, p. 9.

42. "15 Youths Attack Pair on Windsor Street," *Hartford Courant*, October 8, 1956, p. 23.
43. "6 Dallas Youths Hurt," *New York Times*, July 17, 1957, p. 23.
44. "Rock 'n' Roll Fight Hospitalizes Youth," *New York Times*, April 15, 1957, p. 23.
45. "Boy, 15, Stabbed in Battle Among Rock 'n' Roll Fans," *Chicago Tribune*, April 15, 1957, p. A1.
46. "'Rock 'n' Roll' Banned," *New York Times*, September 20, 1956, p. 29.
47. "Rock 'n' Roll Banned in Birmingham," *Los Angeles Sentinel*, July 21, 1960, p. C1.
48. "High Admission Hit by Court After Big Rock 'n' Roll Brawl," *Pittsburgh Courier*, November 30, 1957, p. 44.
49. James Nelson Goodsell, "Rock 'n' Roll Opposition Rises," *Christian Science Monitor*, May 8, 1958, p. 3.
50. Martin and Segrave, p. 36.
51. Jackson, *Big Beat Heat*, p. 194.
52. "Boston Bans R 'n' R After Jam Session Ends in Riot," *Daily Defender*, May 6, 1958, p. A4.
53. Jackson, *Big Beat Heat*, pp. 195, 201.
54. "Rock 'n' Roll King Due to Face Music in Court," *Hartford Courant*, May 12, 1958, p. 19D.
55. Jackson, *Big Beat Heat*, p. 202.
56. Jon Pereles, "The World of Hip-Hop Returns to the Garden," *New York Times*, January 6, 1992, p. C11.
57. Eric Hubler, "Rap Repercussions?," *Washington Post*, August 19, 1986, p. C1.
58. "Eighteen are Arrested After Rap Concert," *New York Times*, July 21, 1986, p. B3.
59. "Teen-Ager Stabbed to Death at Concert," *St. Petersburg Times*, September 12, 1988, p. 4A.
60. Richard Harrington, "On the Beat; No Room to Rap," *Washington Post*, December 13, 1989, p. B7.
61. Karlyn Barker, "DC Police, Crowd Clash Outside Rap Concert," *Washington Post*, November 4, 1991, p. B8.
62. Hubler.
63. Eric Schmitt, "Nassau Coliseum Bans Rap Concerts Till Murder Inquiry Ends," *New York Times*, September 13, 1988, p. B4.
64. Amy Binder, "Constructing Racial Rhetoric: Media Depictions of Harm in Heavy Metal and Rap Music," *American Sociological Review* 58, no. 6 (December 1993), p. 760.
65. "Students, Officers Protest Rap Concert," *Washington Times*, November 25, 1992, p. B2.
66. Jon Pereles, "On Rap, Symbolism and Fear," *New York Times*, February 2, 1992, p. 1.
67. Tricia Rose, "Fear of a Black Planet: Rap Music and Black Cultural Politics in the 1990s," *Journal of Negro Education* 60, no. 3 (Summer 1991), p. 279.
68. Robert S. Ellsworth, *The Fifties Spiritual Marketplace: American Religion in a Decade of Conflict* (New Brunswick, NJ: Rutgers University Press, 1997), p. 16.
69. Jason C. Bivins, *Religion of Fear: The Politics of Horror in Conservative Evangelicalism* (New York: Oxford University Press, 2008), p. 20.
70. Maureen Cleave, "How Does a Beatle Live? John Lennon Lives Like This," *London Evening Standard*, March 4, 1966, www.beatlesinterviews.org/db1966.0304-beatles-john-lennon-were-more-popular-than-jesus-now-maureen-cleave.html.
71. "More Critics Board Beatle 'Ban Wagon,'" *Chicago Tribune*, August 6, 1966, p. D11.
72. "Bas Boast Banning 'Beatles,'" *Pittsburgh Courier*, October 1, 1966, p. 6B.
73. "Beatles Upset the Deep South," *The Guardian*, August 5, 1966, p. 1.
74. "Frantic Fans Mob Beatles in Cleveland," *Los Angeles Times*, August 15, 1966, p. 4.
75. "More Critics Board Beatle 'Ban Wagon.'"
76. "Beatle Mania Hits Sour Note," *Chicago Tribune*, August 5, 1966, p. 3.
77. Frank Newport, "Americans' Church Attendance Inches Up in 2010," Gallup, Inc., June 25, 2010, www.gallup.com/poll/141044/americans-church-attendance-inches-2010.aspx.

78. Ellsworth, pp. 1, 10, 16.
79. "Evangelist to Begin 8-Day Visit," *Hartford Courant*, August 19, 1972, p. 19.
80. Laurence Cohen, "Evangelist Warns Rock Lyrics Harmful," *Hartford Courant*, August 26, 1972, p. 12.
81. Jack Boettner, "Demonstration Triggered by Evangelist," *Los Angeles Times*, May 11, 1979, p. OC A8.
82. "Youthful Faith Will Melt 'Rock,'" *Hartford Courant*, March 28, 1976, p. 1.
83. Bruce Buursma, "Pastors Hold 'Disco Infernos,'" *Chicago Tribune*, October 11, 1980, p. W10.
84. Tom Zito, "Witness of Fire," *Washington Post*, December 3, 1980, p. D1.
85. "On Religion," *Baltimore Sun*, May 8, 1982, p. A12.
86. Theresa Walker, "Ex-Teacher Preaches Evils of Satan in Rock Music," *Los Angeles Times*, April 15, 1984, p. GB5.
87. Mark Forster, "Rock Records Take a Devil of a Beating," *Los Angeles Times*, May 9, 1981, p. SD A1.
88. "California Probes Rock Music 'Devil,'" *Chicago Tribune*, April 29, 1982, p. A2.
89. Bill Billiter, "Satanic Messages Played Back for Assembly Panel," *Los Angeles Times*, April 28, 1982, p. B3.
90. R. Serge Denisoff, *Tarnished Gold: The Record Industry Revisited* (Piscataway, NJ: Transaction Publishers, 1986), p. 408
91. Andrew Epstein, "Did the Devil Make 'em Do It?," *Los Angeles Times*, May 9, 1982, p. J60.
92. "Baby, What'd He Say?," *Washington Post*, December 26, 1982, p. G9.
93. Donna Radcliffe, "Mothers' Group Wants Prince to Clean Up His Act," *Washington Post*, April 23, 1985, p. E2.
94. Ibid.
95. Richard Harrington, "The Capitol Hill Rock War," *Washington Post*, September 20, 1985, p. B1.
96. Karen Sternheimer, *Connecting Social Problems and Popular Culture: Why Media is Not the Answer*, 2nd edition (Boulder, CO: Westview Press, 2013), p. 181.
97. Michael R. Rand, James P. Lynch, and David Cantor, "Criminal Victimization, 1973–95," Bureau of Justice Statistics, National Crime Victimization Survey, 1997, www.prisonpolicy.org/scans/bjs/cv73_95.pdf.
98. Robert W. Blum and Farah Qureshi, "Morbidity and Mortality among Adolescents and Young Adults in the United States," Johns Hopkins University Bloomberg School of Public Health, 2011, www.jhsph.edu/research/centers-and-institutes/center-for-adolescent-health/az/_images/US%20Fact%20Sheet_FINAL.pdf; Centers for Disease Control and Prevention, "Perspectives in Disease Prevention and Health Promotion Suicide—United States, 1970–1980," June 21, 1985, www.cdc.gov/mmwr/preview/mmwrhtml/00000561.htm.
99. "Recording Group Tells of New Step," *New York Times*, November 2, 1985, p. 14.
100. Richard Harrington, "Is Tipper Changing Her Tune?," *Washington Post*, July 22, 1992, p. G7.
101. Nat Hentoff, "The Recording Business, Up Against the Wal-Mart," *Washington Post*, December 7, 1996, p. A25.
102. Gwen Ifill, "Gores Change Tune on Rock-Lyric Hearings," *Washington Post*, November 5, 1987, p. A1.
103. Dawn C. Chmielewski, "Can This Man Save the Music Business?," *Los Angeles Times*, March 9, 2014, p. A1, www.latimes.com/entertainment/envelope/cotown/la-fi-ct-music-business-change-20140309,0,1977338.story#axzz2vxpMlToW.
104. "Resort Bans Rock 'n Roll to Curb Riots," *Los Angeles Times*, July 12, 1956, p. 7.
105. Altschuler, pp. 108, 100.

6

CONCLUSION

Contemporary Pop Culture Crusades

Today it might be difficult to understand why people years ago got so upset about silent-era movies, pinball machines, comic books, and early rock and roll music. Their fears may seem quaint or even prudish by today's standards. It's tempting to think that that stuff was tame, but pop culture today is often much more explicit, and thus things that concern moral crusaders today are significantly *different* from the content people feared in history.

But the previous chapters teach us otherwise: the fears felt by moral crusaders were as much about social change as about content, driven by demographic shifts in immigration, urbanization, and ultimately the changing experiences and expectations of children and teens. Similar factors drive fears of popular culture today. Timing and context are crucial to our understanding of what we are encouraged to fear and who we are told to be afraid of; these "folk devils" we are encouraged to fear become redefined as threats to society writ large and to young people more specifically. We can learn through analyzing the work of moral crusaders how people actively produce meanings of danger and deviance in attempts to enact more social control over a feared—or feared for—group.

Yes, moral crusaders were deeply concerned about the then-new modes of popular culture, but lurking beneath their complaints were fears about how young people used their leisure time and the growth of a new and separate youth-oriented culture. Not coincidentally this expansion of popular culture targeted at youth happened as concerns about juvenile delinquency rose during the twentieth century. The definition of delinquency expanded well beyond youth crime to mean any behavior that was inconsistent with the new expectations of adolescents. No longer in the labor force, teens were expected to remain separate from the "adult" world in ways they hadn't before the turn of the century. This brought new concerns about popular culture, its content, and what young people might be exposed to in this new, separate sphere. The commercialization of leisure was big business, and it meant that traditional influences—such as parents, teachers, and clergy—would have competition.

That competition is ever more visible today, as smartphones allow people to be constantly connected to social media and the internet. We are all familiar with the ubiquitous blank stare into the face of a phone on streets, at the dinner table, in classrooms, and in virtually any public space. *This time*, we may convince ourselves, the threat is more significant. People—young people—can take and send inappropriate photos and videos of themselves or others. They can access content that parents might not approve of and never know about.

New forms of technology have historically created anxieties about their impact on the next generation. Whether movies at the turn of the twentieth century or smartphones at the turn of the twenty-first, the expansion of entertainment choices has caused many to worry that new media will change young people for the worse. With each form of new media, from movies to comic books to music, video games, and social networking, come concerns about the loss of control of information. In the smartphone era, it is virtually impossible to control information or images that anyone can access.

In this chapter, we'll explore contemporary concerns about new media, specifically "sexting," and new ways of conducting moral crusades about new and old media. New media allow very small groups to launch micro crusades that no longer require mass media to spread. For instance, concerns that *Harry Potter* books and movies promote the occult is not a widely held fear, but one that can be sustained across time and space due to the internet and social networking.

While these concerns are very similar to those of the past—about young people, sex, violence, and morality more generally—as we will see, the nature of moral crusading itself has changed due to these new media. No longer is a handful of high-profile, attention-getting crusaders necessary. We can all be moral crusaders now. At the same time, the emotional style of moral crusaders has been adopted by many mainstream news organizations, which no longer need to rely on covering a moral crusade for content. They can create crusade-style stories for the sake of an attention-grabbing, dramatic story itself.

From Moral Crusaders to Moral Profiteers

Historically, moral crusaders had to be able to get public attention in a limited media environment. At the beginning of the twentieth century, this meant landing public speaking engagements, getting newspaper coverage, and delivering radio addresses. Later, mid-century crusaders could get national audience attention if they received television coverage, as the anti-comic book and anti-rock activists sometimes could.

This meant that many of those who managed to get media attention were already in positions of power, even on a small scale, and were at least on the radar as newsmakers. Politicians—mayors and members of Congress and their spouses—might not have been the first to be concerned about movie content, pinball machines, comic books, or rock music, but they could easily use both the issue and their positions of power to gain attention and also make legal changes to support the cause.

Those not in politics had to be skilled at getting media attention, by writing books and giving lectures or sermons, riding the crest of rising concerns about popular culture. As Howard Becker explains, moral crusaders don't have to be powerful leaders, but their crusades often provide them with elevated status as experts.[1] Psychiatrist Frederic Wertham became a public intellectual after his writing appeared in popular magazines, widely publicizing his condemnation of comic books, as well as his appearance at Senate hearings. Asa Carter, already getting media attention in his fight against desegregation, used his claims about rock and roll as a tool of integration to create a leadership position for himself in a local white supremacist group. Anti-rock preachers likely earned more speaking engagements following media coverage of their claims. Getting the attention of reporters made a big difference.

But in the twenty-first century, the traditional media gatekeepers are less important. Social media such as YouTube, Facebook, and Twitter now make it easier for practically anyone to become a moral crusader, albeit with varying degrees of success. Besides posting videos, pictures, or blog posts, anyone can forward links to people in their networks to raise awareness about anything. Anyone can leave comments advocating a cause anywhere, even if the site they comment on is only tangentially related (or not at all related) to their cause. However, crusaders may find it harder to reach a mass audience as media audiences become more segmented. Micro crusades can gain steam through social media without the attention or awareness of much of the public, targeting an already sympathetic but small group.

And as cable news seeks to stay "relevant" in today's new media environment, producers often turn to social media for story ideas. It's no longer necessary for a moral crusader to pitch a story idea to an editor via press release or to be interviewed by a reporter to get attention. Instead, traditional media might follow new media's lead if a video "goes viral" or a comment is retweeted enough for a traditional news organization to do a story on the topic, generating more attention without the need for a high-profile moral crusader.

There has possibly never been a better time to launch a moral crusade, from a media perspective. News programming trades heavily in emotion, borrowing tactics from traditional moral crusaders in order to keep viewers' attention, hoping to get click-throughs, comments, and retweets for their content. No longer limited by broadcast time, the internet requires that traditional news outlets constantly produce content—and constantly attract consumers.

This means that many stories might take on the *style* of a moral crusade without the direction of a moral crusader, or even a desired outcome such as a policy change. Instead, many news organizations have become moral profiteers, essentially using moral outrage as a ratings-grabbing tool.[2] Like traditional moral crusaders, their arguments are largely emotional, focusing on fears of social change and condemning a "folk devil" that is allegedly to blame. And these fears are often dramatically out of proportion with the actual threat this group or so-called problem poses. Less interested in reporting on facts or putting fears in context, many news organizations draw on existing concerns their target audience might share in order to yield a larger audience.

Sexting: A Crusaderless Crusade

Take "sexting," for example: a catchy word tailor-made for infotainment parading as news. Sexting entails sending either sexually charged images, videos, or words via text message; the word seems to have first been used by an Australian newspaper in 2005 while describing an unfaithful athlete whose steamy text messages were later discovered.[3] It was certainly not the first story to discuss the sexually explicit text messages; the tabloid-driven Australian and British presses were full of stories about such texts before these kinds of reports became more prevalent in the US. Early stories about texting mainly focused on sex scandals in the UK, most notably claims of soccer star David Beckham's alleged infidelity in 2004, with explicit texts supposedly sent to other women.

Concern about sexting spread without formal moral crusaders; unlike earlier concerns about popular culture, sexting did not need media savvy people in leadership positions to raise awareness. All it took was editors and producers looking for a "hot topic" to lead to the appearance of a new trend. Sexting became a common-sense problem, one that many people thought was a new teen issue because we so frequently heard that it was. In 2011, the term entered the Oxford English Dictionary, cementing its place as a "permanent" practice and source of concern.

The press had a few misses before creating the catchy term. A 2001 British book review included the term "textual intercourse," but it didn't catch on.[4] The clumsier phrase "sex texts" appeared in multiple 2002 UK newspaper stories focusing on gossipy scandals among betrayed lovers who learned of their partner's infidelity by viewing their text messages.[5] The phrase, or its inversion, "text sex," appeared in numerous articles in the British press that year, including a letter to an advice columnist about a woman having "hot text sex with a colleague."[6] "Sex text pest" also became a popular tabloid headline to describe unwanted sexually explicit texts. A London *Daily Telegraph* story used the term "intexicated" to describe texts sent while drunk that senders later regretted.[7] News accounts occasionally reported on adult sexual predators using text messaging to try to lure young people, but mainly focused on adult indiscretions.

According to industry data, the number of text messages sent monthly in the US grew from 1.2 billion in 2003 to 75 billion in 2008.[8] As texting became a more common form of communication in the US, both interest in and stories about text messages—and their potential downside—became more frequent, and stories began to focus more on the potential danger texting might pose to young people.

In 2009, stories about sexting increased dramatically in the US when several teens in Pennsylvania faced child pornography charges after sending images of themselves to classmates; the recipients also faced charges.[9] (One story referred to the group charged as the "sexting six."[10]) Headlines like "'Sexting' Disturbing New Trend Among Teens" and "Sexting Has Become a Dangerous Trend" appeared across the country, largely in response to reports about the Pennsylvania case.[11] Similar to what sociologists Craig Reinarman and Harry Levine describe as "the routinization of caricature," news coverage framed the Pennsylvania case as typical rather than exceptional.[12] "Parents Urged to Explain Sexting Risks to Kids," "'Sexting' Case Hits Local Family," "Latest Teen Craze," "Tips, Warning Signs Kids May Be Sexting," and "Poll: Teen Sexting is on the Rise" are just a few of the more than 2,200 newspaper stories about sexting that appeared in 2009 alone.[13] Sexting represented the double-edged fear adults have about young people, viewing them as both victims and perpetrators: at once too naïve to know the consequences of their actions and also too sexually knowing for adult comfort.

This story attracted the attention of cable news and morning news chat shows, with legal experts weighing in, warning on the airwaves and in the newspapers across the country of the dangers of teen sexting. A few weeks later, John Sheehan, of the National Center for Missing and Exploited Children, commented to a reporter that "we're seeing sexting more and more," leading to concerns of a new and dangerous trend.[14]

Was it a new and dangerous trend? There was very little if any data on the subject initially. Drawing on a 2008 survey conducted by the National Campaign to Prevent Teen and Unplanned Pregnancy, several articles focused on the finding that 20 percent of teens said that they had sent "nude or semi-nude" images of themselves via text or posted them online (33 percent of young adults responded that they had sent such images as well).[15] A *USA Today* headline warned "Survey: 1 in 5 Teens 'Sext' Despite Risks," reporting, ominously, that "of teens who sext, 80% are under 18" (disregarding the fact that *most* teens are in fact under 18).[16] An *Irish Times* headline claimed that in Ireland one third of all students receive "sexts."[17] Unlike early stories in the UK and Australia, in the US sexting stories focused almost exclusively on youth. It's likely that the news coverage of sexting led polling organizations to conduct surveys, which led to more news about sexting.

Police and school officials have worked to raise awareness about this issue as it has affected their communities. But rather than the result of the work of specific moral crusaders, concerns about sexting spread through the ubiquity of these stories, with experts recruited to add gravitas to news reports.

People who make their living as parenting experts could capitalize on the sexting coverage, marketing this new topic of focus. "Expert to Explain 'Sexting,' How to Deal with it," the *Salem News* reported. "There are so many younger kids that are doing this," claimed Joani Geltman, a social worker who provides "coaching" services and hosts "ask the expert parties" for parents. She said that "parents are just freaked out" and that she had received many calls since the original story about the "sexting six" broke.[18] The definition of parenting expertise was easily stretched. People with parenting blogs could be billed as "parenting experts" for stories on sexting, as in a *San Jose Mercury News* story featuring the advice of blogger turned author Amy Lupold Bair, who suggests a "no tolerance policy for dangerous behaviors."[19] But these are not necessarily moral crusaders; they are not activists championing a cause or demanding that legislation be written to restrict teens' cell phone use. I have personally been asked to comment on this issue many times. I suspect that many other scholars, therapists, counselors, and self-proclaimed parenting experts were likewise recruited into this topic, rather than independent champions of a moral crusade against sexting.

The rise in coverage of sexting stories led to debates about legal issues. Those charged with possessing or distributing child pornography in some cases have had to register as sex offenders, while adults would not be subject to similar penalties for the same behavior, assuming the image was of an adult. Those penalized were often the same people prosecutors said they were trying to protect, to dissuade teens from sending images of themselves, leading to question whether one can be both a perpetrator and victim if the images sent were of themselves.[20]

Some parents and critics—including the American Civil Liberties Union (ACLU)—challenged that criminalizing young people for making what is clearly a big mistake was overkill.[21] "Misguided teens should not be punished with laws meant to protect them—as child pornography laws are supposed to do," the *Christian Science Monitor* editorialized.[22]

Several states have proposed bills to make sharing "suggestive photos" between teens a crime, but distinct from child pornography laws, decriminalizing the recipient as long as they did not seek out an image and as long as they make reasonable efforts to delete them. Sexting's legal gray area serves as a reminder of how quickly the technology landscape changes, and how these changes trigger fears of new media and youth, and old fears of sexuality and youth.

The rise in concerns about sexting ironically corresponds with declines in teen pregnancy, which reached historic lows in 2009.[23] Rates of sexual activity among teens were essentially flat over the 20-year period as well.[24] But the public seldom hears about these trends; they don't make for compelling or dramatic news, unlike the stories of teens who may have posted revealing pictures of themselves or others on Facebook or other social media. And as social media scholar danah boyd points out, we have created so much control over young people that social media is one of their few bastions of relative freedom. "Given the array of restrictions teens face, it's not surprising that they have embraced technology with such enthusiasm," boyd remarked, noting that in the past children and teens walked to school, roamed their neighborhoods, and worked with far less parental supervision.[25]

Schools around the country held assemblies for students and meetings for parents about the emerging issue that year. Should students who received photos—but did not seek them out—have their phones confiscated?[26] Was this normal teen behavior? Was every teen now sexting?

A Pew Research Internet Project survey conducted in late 2009 found that only 4 percent of teens sent such images; other polls conducted that year found 9 and 10 percent sent revealing images of themselves.[27] Hidden in the anxiety-laden coverage was the fact that the surveys indicated that the vast majority of teens—between 80 and 96 percent—*did not* send sexually explicit images of themselves. But by then it was too late; while not all the survey results were alarming, it didn't stop the alarmist tone of sexting news reports. Sexting stories constructed this as a widespread and growing teen problem, one that parents had better pay attention to and caution their kids against.

Since the term "sexting" was relatively new—as was smartphone technology and cell service with enough bandwidth to send images—it could easily seem like a new problem, which in turn seemed to pose a new and growing threat. And as young people became more visibly associated with smartphones, sexting became seen as a teen problem. But a 2014 Pew Research Center report found that 25–34-year-olds were more likely than other age groups to send sexually suggestive images.[28] There are numerous high-profile examples of adult sexting, including then-representative and one-time New York mayoral candidate Anthony Weiner's and former quarterback Brett Favre's crotch shots. But the idea that this is a youth problem has been cemented in the public imagination.

That the vast majority of teens did not "sext" became less important than the fact that they hypothetically *could* send or post revealing images of themselves. New media offered a potential moral pitfall for current and future young people, news reports claimed, with images very difficult or impossible to "unsend." Yes, sending such images is clearly a bad idea at any age—as they can easily be reappropriated, posted online, and are nearly impossible to control—but the concerns about sexting are about more than the mistake itself, and instead are about the access to creating and receiving information and images beyond adult control.

Sexting fears also correspond with declines in traditional media; newspapers continue to struggle with declining circulations, as they and television news networks have to find ways to become profitable online. Scandal, gossip, and sex have been and remain prime subjects to lure viewers. Ironically, the very technology that readers were encouraged to fear helped to create the ubiquitous stories about sexting. In hopes of drawing click-throughs, posted links, and retweets, news sites encourage visitors to share their opinions; a sexting story can generate many comments and moral outrage, now the often lifeblood of commercial news sites. Unlike traditional moral crusaders who hope to restrict a particular type of media content, moral profiteers do not. In fact, they benefit from the moral outrage they suspect audiences will feel. Rather than look for resolution, in some ways old and new media benefit from sexting. The more outrageous or disturbing the story, the better.

Micro Crusades: Anti-*Harry Potter* Activists

New media can also help smaller crusades, particularly those without high-profile crusaders or the support of traditional mass media. When J. K. Rowling's *Harry Potter* books became runaway best sellers in the late 1990s, and then a blockbuster film series beginning in 2001, some parents and church leaders complained that the boy wizard promoted the occult and Satanism to young readers.[29] Readers seemed enraptured with the books and character, attending themed parties in costume to celebrate each book's release, leading a small but vocal group to wonder if children would imitate Harry and perform witchcraft themselves.

The series became the most banned or challenged book of the 2000s, according to the American Library Association.[30]

In 2004, a Plano, Texas, parent sued a school district for holding a *Harry Potter* party at an elementary school, claiming that doing so served as an endorsement of the Wicca religion. The *Dallas Morning News* reported on his claim as isolated: "one parent's attempt." The parent based his claims on information he found from an internet search.[31]

This is an example of how the internet allows contemporary crusades to become micro crusades. Websites allow people who might support a moral crusade to learn about the supposed problem, take action, and then discuss and share the issue with their social networks. Like-minded others can publically "like" ideas on pages linked to Facebook and easily post links to their own websites or social media accounts. And with niche cable programming, moral crusades that might not be taken seriously by producers on most channels might find a home. For instance, the website for the Christian Broadcasting Network (CBN) includes a page on "The *Harry Potter* Controversy" and includes numerous stories about the topic on its website.[32]

While many people might not even know that moral crusades against the *Harry Potter* series exist, a smaller, targeted group can be well-versed in the claims. This might not lead to new legislation or any sort of change, but it does serve as a tool to help smaller groups define themselves. For some, rejecting *Harry Potter* is a way to embrace Christianity and possibly define those who don't as outsiders, part of what they may view as a disturbing secular culture that must be guarded against.

Micro crusades don't need mass media or a mass audience, although they might get both in the form of curious onlookers. By defining their audience more specifically, activists seeking to warn like-minded others can provide easily accessible information without having to go through the trouble of having a book published or getting a news interview. Their potential to create change and redefine meanings of deviance might be much more limited, but it exists for a subset of the population who are amenable to their claims.

Critics such as Richard Abanes, who published *Harry Potter and the Bible: The Menace Behind the Magick* in 2001, worried that young fans would adopt witchcraft as a way of life. "Harry Potter has real-world occult parallels… the books present astrology, numerology mediumship, crystal gazing… kids like to copy." According to activist Jon Watkins, "Satan is up to his old tricks again, and the main focus is the children of the world." Watkins also claimed that "the whole purpose of these books is to desensitize readers and introduce them to the occult."[33]

Echoing concerns about satanic messages in rock music, the popularity of the books caused some religious activists to fear that readers would worship the character Harry Potter, and turn to the use of magic. But unlike the anti-rock crusades of the 1980s, no attempts at high-profile legislation followed.

Like the coverage of backwards masking in the 1980s, the alleged practice of putting secret backwards messages in music, coverage of *Harry Potter*'s critics was mostly skeptical. According to a 2013 Harris Poll, 26 percent of Americans said they believe in witches: a surprisingly large number, but still a minority (and some of these believers might practice Wicca and do not believe that witches are dangerous).[34]

Unlike the scores of news accounts reporting on crusades against movies, pinball, comic books, or music, the anti-*Harry Potter* crusades drew fewer stories. News stories that appeared tended to downplay the threat. The *Dallas Morning News* described activists as "a small legion of conservative Christian critics," and added that "more than 50 million copies [of the *Harry Potter* books] are in print worldwide. There has been no evidence of widespread conversions to paganism or witchcraft."[35] Most stories in traditional newspapers also seemed dubious about critics' claims. "In this day and age, Harry Potter is the least of our problems," wrote a *Dallas Morning News* columnist in 2001, referring to the attacks on September 11 of that year, and the emerging war on terror and weak economy that followed.[36]

A *USA Today* story places criticism of *Harry Potter* in context with other highly popular classic books, such as Maya Angelou's *I Know Why the Caged Bird Sings* and Mark Twain's *Adventures of Huckleberry Finn*, noting that these and other books continually have calls for removal from libraries.[37] A New York *Daily News* story, derisively titled "Holy Rollers Raise Cain," skeptically reports on claims that the famous scar on Harry's forehead is actually an "S" for "Satan." The article concludes by noting that other Christian groups, including the Italian Conference of Catholic Bishops, defend the stories as admirable battles of good against evil.[38] A number of Christian activists spoke out in support of the books, making the case that the story is a parable, finding theological themes in their pages.[39]

Moral Crusades: Past, Present, and Future

New forms of media practically assure the continuation of moral crusades about popular culture—they both create anxieties about change and provide new tools to disseminate information about the new technology's alleged dangers. As we have seen throughout this book, even if the focus of concern moves on to a new target, at the heart of anti-pop culture crusades lie anxieties about social change and changes in childhood and adolescence.

Like tides that ebb and flow, so do moral crusades and the moral panics that sometimes follow. Fears may rise when the confluence of events creates a breaking point of tolerance. For instance, the confluence of immigration, urbanization, and cultural changes in the early twentieth century created fear that the country was changing too much and too fast, and moral crusaders could easily point to movies as visibly coinciding with all of these shifts.

As representatives of an unknown future, moral crusaders can easily highlight concerns about children, both as potential victims and villains. Pinball machines and comic books seemed scary at a time when children and teens had more leisure time than ever, and fears about wartime and postwar delinquency rose, as did concerns about organized crime. As racial segregation began to legally dismantle, rock and roll's popularity pointed to not just a change in musical taste but in the racial order as well. Concerns about sex, violence, and the secularization of American life are also reflected in crusades against music.

At the heart of pop culture crusades also lies the contested meaning of free speech at a time when our media environment has dramatically reduced the power of gatekeepers. Moral crusaders succeeded in part during the twentieth century: movies had censors and then a code, pinball machines were banned, comic books had a code, and music had parental warning labels. But the victories were clearly temporary. Those twentieth-century solutions no longer work in the digital age, when video, games, text, and music can all be easily shared. Thus, moral crusades and moral panics can easily re-emerge in response to these changes.

With the expansion of entertainment choices over the past century, older forms of media have to compete with newer, typically more individualized media options. This means to draw audiences, content constantly pushes boundaries to get our attention. And as media has increasingly become niche-oriented, there is less of an expectation that all movies, games, books, or music must be "suitable" for all audiences and age levels. These market forces, coupled with new technologies and legal decisions supporting freedom of expression, have made regulating content virtually impossible today.

Moral crusades are instructive: they teach us about how and why individuals and groups work in reactionary ways in response to change, about the tools they use to do so, and about the contexts in which they couch their concerns. Moral crusades are ultimately about attempts at control over a group that is feared and/or feared for. As the meanings of childhood and adolescence have mutated dramatically over the past century, children and teens have become a potent source of fear and concern, and a ripe subject for moral crusaders.

While we might understand the motivation of moral crusaders and the underlying reasons when the public responds in the form of a moral panic, it is important to note that moral panics are highly problematic. They are often based on misinformation, as the fear generated is disproportionate. Moral panics feed on emotional rather than rational responses, and thus create problematic changes posing as "solutions." The most dramatic example would be Prohibition, which outlawed the sale of alcohol in the United States from 1920 to 1933, creating the foundation for organized crime and an almost impossible task for law enforcement when a large swath of the population became de facto criminals. On a smaller scale, the anti-movie crusades led first to police censorship and later to a power-hungry and openly anti-Semitic Joseph

Breen determining "suitable" movie content almost singlehandedly. Not only does this call into question the role of free speech, but also who has the power to determine what content is acceptable in a multicultural and rapidly changing society.

Studying past moral crusades against popular culture gives us the opportunity to fully understand how large-scale economic changes have played a role in concerns about popular culture in the past so that we might understand the present and future better. The next time we hear that shocking acts of violence are the fault of some new form of entertainment, we can go beyond the emotional outcry and think critically about the broader context of complaints about popular culture.

We can ask who might benefit from being a moral crusader: how might they achieve more power, how might their crusade elevate their status? And most importantly, who are they hoping to restrict? Why are groups that we come to define as problem populations (whether they be creators or consumers of a criticized form of popular culture) defined as such? And much like the aftermath of the 1990s video game panic, we can study the impact of the new regulations and forms of social control. Often the groups with the least social power end up bearing the largest burden of social control; calls for more severe punishment of juveniles following the panic have not been applied uniformly, as males of color from lower income families are more likely to experience criminalization in their schools and community. Far from benign attempts at improving society, moral crusades often have dire consequences for already marginalized groups—even if this was not the intention of the crusaders themselves.

Some of the crusades of the past likely seem absurd today; likewise, some of our own concerns will likely seem misguided in the future with the benefit of time. But at the time, some people were really afraid of pinball, were convinced that comic books were a major threat, and thought demonic messages were secretly inserted into pop music. Rather than just dismiss these moral panics as foolish, it is important to think about the power we have attributed to popular culture in the past and present.

Does the pleasure of its consumption steer people away from more "serious" cultural pursuits, or distract from economic productivity? In condemning something that is popular and enjoyed by a wide audience rather than the privileged few, crusades against popular culture are ultimately an attempt to shore up "high culture" by condemning what becomes defined as "low culture." These cultural distinctions create status, as sociologist Pierre Bourdieu notes.[40] Reinforcing these distinctions through moral crusades further derides the status of those who might enjoy a now debased form of popular culture. Often this cultural hierarchy is used to create status distinctions between generations, as shifts in the experiences of children and adolescents may make these groups seem unrecognizable to the experiences just one generation before.

Moral panics also divert us from what really causes the problems we have been told popular culture produces. Media content seems a simple—yet always visible—representation of concerns about sex, violence, and morality as a whole. Its purpose is to amuse, distract, shock, fascinate—anything to get our attention for profit. While moral crusaders may be well-intentioned, and many of us might share their disdain for a variety of media content, unfortunately they discourage us from going beyond superficial explanations for issues that concern so many people. For instance, the underlying causes of teen pregnancy may seem on the surface to be related to sex-laden popular culture, but there are significant explanations rooted in socio-economic status. The problems of poverty, for instance, and how and why these problems may produce violent communities go unnoticed by a large swath of the public, heavily focused on popular culture.

But crusades against popular culture are likely here to stay. They draw attention for their crusaders, play on existing concerns about both social change and media content, and allow us to express moral judgment about others in the public sphere. Moral crusades draw on emotion; the sociological perspective asks us to look deeper to better understand both those who are feared and those who are feared for, as well as the moral crusaders themselves.

Notes

1. Howard Becker, *Outsiders: Studies in the Sociology of Deviance* (New York: Free Press, 1963).
2. This phrase originated with my colleague, Brady Potts, during a conversation on March 25, 2014.

3. Yvonne Roberts, "The One and Only," *Sunday Telegraph Magazine* (Sydney), July 31, 2005, p. 22.

4. Rachel Holmes, "The Joy of Textual Intercourse," Book Review, *Guardian Weekly*, March 14, 2001, p. 18.

5. Scott Douglas, "My Sex Text Revenge," *Daily Record*, January 19, 2002, p. 1; Paul Harris, "Mobile Users Scammed in Sex Text Messages Scam," *The Observer*, January 20, 2002, p. 11.

6. Joan Burnie, "Just Joan: The Agony Aunt with the Answers," *Daily Record*, March 27, 2002, p. 32.

7. Becky Barrow, "Phone Blunders by the 'Intexicated,'" *Daily Telegraph* (London), December 20, 2003, p. 5.

8. TextServe, www.textserv.com, industry data from The Wireless Association.

9. Bob Styles, "Teens Face Porn Charges in 'Sexting,'" *Tribune-Review* (Greensburg, PA), January 13, 2009.

10. Mike Seate, "Sexting Arrests Provide Warning," *Pittsburgh Tribune Review*, February 3, 2009.

11. "'Sexting' Disturbing New Trend Among Teens," *The Star Phoenix* (Saskatoon, Saskatchewan), March 26, 2009, p. D7; "Not Child's Play," *The Record* (Bergen County, NJ), April 10, 2009, p. A20.

12. Craig Reinarman and Harry Levine (eds.). *Crack in America: Demon Drugs and Social Justice* (Berkeley: University of California Press, 1997), p. 24.

13. Based on a Lexis-Nexis search. Jeff Ducharme, "Parents Urged to Explain the Sexting Risks to Kids," *The Telegraph-Journal* (New Brunswick), July 28, 2009, p. C4; Angeljean Chiaramida, "'Sexting' Case Hits Local Family," *The Daily News of Newburyport* (Massachusetts), June 27, 2009; Beatriz E. Valenzuela, "Latest Teen Craze: Sexting," *Daily Press—Victorville* (California), September 6, 2009; "Poll: Teen Sexting is on the Rise," *The Tampa Tribune* (Florida), December 4, 2009, p. 1.

14. Bob Styles, "'Sexting' Happening 'More and More,'" *Tribune-Review* (Greensburg, PA), February 2, 2009.

15. The National Campaign to Prevent Teen and Unplanned Pregnancy, "Sex and Tech Summary: Results from a Survey of Teens and Young Adults," http://thenationalcampaign.org/sites/default/files/resource-primary-download/sex_and_tech_summary.pdf, 2008, p. 1.

16. Donna Leinwand, "Survey: 1 in 5 Teens 'Sext' Despite Risks," *USA Today*, June 24, 2009, p. 3A.

17. "One Third of Pupils Being Sent 'Sexts,' Parents Told," *Irish News*, August 4, 2009, p. 21.

18. Cate Lecuyer, "Expert to Explain 'Sexting,' How to Deal with it," *Salem News* (Beverly, MA), May 21, 2009; http://joanigeltman.com.

19. Angela Hill, "Five Tips For a Family Digital Contract," *San Jose Mercury News*, June 26, 2013; http://resourcefulmommy.com/about-resourceful-mommy.

20. Talia Buford, "State Trying to Clarify Sexting," *Providence Journal*, January 17, 2010, p. 1; Marsha Levick, "Sexting Bill Victimizes Pennsylvania Teens," *Patriot-News*, October 23, 2012, www.pennlive.com/opinion/index.ssf/2012/10/sexting_bill_victimizes_pennsylvania_teens.html.

21. Erin L. Nissley, "ACLU Sues Wyoming County DA over 'Sexting' Case," *Times-Tribune* (Scranton, PA), March 27, 2009.

22. Editorial, "'Sexting' Overreach," *Christian Science Monitor*, April 28, 2009, p. 8.

23. Child Trends Databank, "Indicators on Children and Youth: Teen Pregnancy," December 2013, www.childtrends.org/?indicators=teen-pregnancy.

24. Child Trends Databank, "Indicators on Children and Youth: Sexually Active Teens," December 2013, www.childtrends.org/?indicators=sexually-active-teens; Child Trends

Databank, "Indicators on Children and Youth: Sexually Experienced Teens," December 2013, www.childtrends.org/?indicators=sexually-experienced-teens.

25. danah boyd, "Whether it's Bikes or Bytes, Teens are Teens," *Los Angeles Times*, April 13, 2014, p. A19. (Note that boyd spells her name with lowercase letters.)

26. Teresa Ann Boeckel, "Parents Raise Concerns About Sexting," *York Daily Record* (Pennsylvania), April 16, 2009.

27. Amanda Lenhart, "Teens and Sexting," Pew Research Internet Project, Pew Research Center, December 15, 2009, www.pewinternet.org/2009/12/15/teens-and-sexting.

28. Amanda Lenhart and Maeve Duggan, "Couples, the Internet, and Social Media," Pew Research Center, February 11, 2014, www.pewinternet.org/2014/02/11/main-report-30.

29. For more discussion, see Henry Jenkins, *Convergence Culture: Where Old and New Media Collide* (New York: New York University Press, 2006), Chapter 5.

30. American Library Association, "Top 100 Banned/Challenged Books 2000–2009," www.ala.org/bbooks/top-100-bannedchallenged-books-2000-2009. A challenged book is not necessarily banned, but one that receives complaints and requests to ban.

31. Linda Stewart Ball, "Harry Potter Party Can Go on at School," *Dallas Morning News*, April 15, 2004, p. 1B.

32. www.cbn.com/special/harrypotter.

33. Anthony Breznican, "Christians Square Off Over Harry Potter," *Dallas Morning News*, November 10, 2001, p. 5G.

34. Harris Polls, "Americans Belief in God, Miracles and Heaven Declines," December 16, 2013, www.harrisinteractive.com/NewsRoom/HarrisPolls/tabid/447/ctl/ReadCustom%20Default/mid/1508/ArticleId/1353/Default.aspx.

35. Breznican.

36. James Ragland, "The Devil and Mr. Potter," *Dallas Morning News*, November 30, 2001, p. 1C.

37. Jacqueline Blais, "Not Everyone's Wild About Harry Potter," *USA Today*, September 11, 2003, p. 4D.

38. Bill Bell, "Holy Rollers Raise Cain," *Daily News*, July 2, 2000, p. 4.

39. Nancy Churnin, "Harry Earns his Wings," *Dallas Morning News*, July 17, 2005, p. 1E.

40. Pierre Bourdieu, *Distinction: A Social Critique of the Judgment of Taste* (Cambridge, MA: Harvard University Press, 1984).

SELECTED BIBLIOGRAPHY

Altschuler, Glenn C. *All Shook Up: How Rock 'n' Roll Changed America.* New York: Oxford University Press, 2003.

Balko, Radley. "The Subversive Vending Machine," *Reason*, June 2010.

Beaty, Bart. *Fredric Wertham and the Critique of Mass Culture.* Jackson, MS: University Press of Mississippi, 2005.

Becker, Howard. *Outsiders: Studies in the Sociology of Deviance.* New York: Free Press, 1963.

Bernstein, Lee. *The Greatest Menace: Organized Crime in Cold War America.* Boston: University of Massachusetts Press, 2002.

Bernstein, Matthew. *Controlling Hollywood: Censorship and Regulation in the Studio Era.* Brunswick, NJ: Rutgers University Press, 1999.

Best, Joel. *Social Problems*, 2nd edition. New York: W.W. Norton and Company, 2012.

—— *Random Violence: How We Talk About New Crimes and New Victims.* Berkeley: University of California Press, 1999.

Binder, Amy. "Constructing Racial Rhetoric: Media Depictions of Harm in Heavy Metal and Rap Music." *American Sociological Review* 58, no. 6 (December 1993), pp. 753–767.

Birnbaum, Larry. *Before Elvis: The Prehistory of Rock 'n' Roll.* Lanham, MD: Scarecrow Press, 2013.

Bivins, Jason C. *Religion of Fear: The Politics of Horror in Conservative Evangelicalism.* New York: Oxford University Press, 2008.

Black, Gregory D. *Hollywood Censored: Morality Codes, Catholics, and the Movies.* New York: Cambridge University Press, 1994.

Bourdieu, Pierre. *Distinction: A Social Critique of the Judgment of Taste.* Cambridge, MA: Harvard University Press, 1984.

Brodkin, Karen. *How Jews Became White Folks and What That Says About Race in America.* New Brunswick, NJ: Rutgers University Press, 1998.

Burnham, John C. *Bad Habits: Drinking, Smoking, Taking Drugs, Gambling, Sexual Misbehavior and Swearing in American History.* New York, New York University Press, 1993.

Burns, Ronald and Charles Crawford. "School Shootings, the Media, and Public Fear: Ingredients for a Moral Panic." *Crime, Law, and Social Change* 32 (1999), pp. 147–168.

Burnstein, Daniel Eli. *Next to Godliness: Confronting Dirt and Despair in Progressive Era New York City.* Champaign, IL: University of Illinois Press, 2006.

Chase, William Sheafe. *Catechism on Motion Pictures in Inter-State Commerce.* Nabu Press, 2012 [1922].

Cohen, Stanley. *Folk Devils and Moral Panics*, 3rd edition. New York: Routledge, 2002.

Critcher, Chas. *Moral Panics and the Media.* Philadelphia: Open University Press, 2003.

Daniels, Les. *Comix: A History of Comic Books in America*. New York: Bonanza Books, 1971.

de Young, Mary. *The Day Care Ritual Abuse Moral Panic*. Jefferson, NC: McFarland & Company Publishers, 2004.

Duncan, Randy and Matthew J. Smith. *The Power of Comics: History, Form and Culture*. New York: Continuum, 2009.

Ellsworth, Robert S. *The Fifties Spiritual Marketplace: American Religion in a Decade of Conflict*. New Brunswick, NJ: Rutgers University Press, 1997.

Erickson, Kai T. *Wayward Puritans: A Study in the Sociology of Deviance*, revised edition. Upper Saddle River, NJ: Prentice-Hall, 2004.

Facey, Paul W. *The Legion of Decency: A Sociological Analysis of the Emergence and Development of a Social Pressure Group*. New York: Arno Press, 1945.

Gans, Herbert J. *Popular Culture and High Culture: An Analysis and Evaluation of Taste*. New York: Basic Books, 1974.

Gilbert, James. "Mass Culture and the Fear of Delinquency." *Journal of Early Adolescence*, 5 (1985), pp. 505–516.

——— *A Cycle of Outrage: America's Reaction to the Juvenile Delinquent in the 1950s*. New York: Oxford University Press, 1986.

Glassner, Barry. *The Culture of Fear: Why Americans Are Afraid of the Wrong Things*. New York: Basic Books, 1999.

Goode, Erich and Nachman Ben-Yehuda. *Moral Panics: The Social Construction of Deviance*. Cambridge, MA: Blackwell, 1994.

Gorman, Joseph Bruce. *Kefauver: A Political Biography*. New York: Oxford University Press, 1971.

Grieveson, Lee. *Policing Cinema: Movies and Censorship in Early-Twentieth Century America*. Berkeley: University of California Press, 2004.

Hajdu, David. *The Ten-Cent Plague: The Great Comic Book Scare and How it Changed America*. New York: Farrar, Straus, and Giroux, 2008.

Heer, Jeet and Kent Worcester (eds.). *A Comic Studies Reader*. Jackson, MS: University Press of Mississippi, 2009.

Heins, Marjorie. *Not in Front of the Children: Indecency, Censorship, and the Innocence of Youth*, 2nd edition. New Brunswick, NJ: Rutgers University Press, 2007.

Jackson, John A. *Big Beat Heat: Alan Freed and the Early Years of Rock and Roll*. New York: Schirmer Books, 1991.

Jeffers, H. Paul. *The Napoleon of New York: Mayor Fiorello H. La Guardia*. New York: Wiley, 2002.

Jenkins, Henry. *Convergence Culture: Where Old and New Media Collide*. New York: New York University Press, 2006.

Kessner, Thomas. *Fiorello H. La Guardia and the Making of Modern New York*. New York: McGraw-Hill, 1989.

Kidd, Dustin. *Pop Culture Freaks: Identity, Mass Media, and Society*. Boulder, CO: Westview Press, 2014.

Lears, Jackson. *Something for Nothing: Luck in America*. New York: Viking Books, 2003.

Longstreet, Stephen. *Win or Lose: A Social History of Gambling*. Indianapolis: The Bobbs-Merrill Company, Inc., 1977.

Lopes, Paul. *Demanding Respect: The Evolution of the American Comic Book*. Philadelphia: Temple University Press, 2009.

Males, Mike A. *Framing Youth: Ten Myths About the Next Generation*. Monroe, ME: Common Courage Press, 1999.

Manning, Peter K. and Bonnie Campbell. "Pinball as Game, Fad, and Synecdoche." *Youth and Society* 4 (1973), pp. 333–358.

Martin, Linda and Kerry Segrave. *Anti-Rock: The Opposition to Rock 'n' Roll*. New York: Da Capo Press, 1993.

McClellan, George B. *The Gentleman and the Tiger: The Autobiography of George B. McClellan, Jr.* New York: Lippincott, 1956.

Nasaw, David. *Children of the City: At Work and at Play*. New York: Anchor Books, 2012.

Reinarman, Craig. "The Social Construction of Drug Scares." In P. Adler and P. Adler (eds.) *Constructions of Deviance: Social Power, Context, and Interaction* (Belmont, CA: Wadsworth Publishing, 1994), pp. 92–105.

Reinarman, Craig and Harry Levine (eds.). *Crack in America: Demon Drugs and Social Justice*. Berkeley: University of California Press, 1997.

Reppetto, Thomas. *Bringing Down the Mob*. New York: Henry Holt and Company, 2006.

Rose, Tricia. "Fear of a Black Planet: Rap Music and Black Cultural Politics in the 1990s." *Journal of Negro Education* 60, no. 3 (Summer 1991), pp. 276–290.

Ross, Steven J. *Working-Class Hollywood: Silent Film and the Shaping of Class in America*. Princeton, NJ: Princeton University Press, 1998.

Schlosser, Eric. *Reefer Madness: Sex, Drugs, and Cheap Labor in the American Black Market*. Boston: Houghton Mifflin, 2003.

Sklar, Robert. *Movie-Made America: A Cultural History of the Movies*. New York: Vintage Books, 1975.

Springhall, John. *Youth, Popular Culture and Moral Panics: Penny Gaffs to Gangsta-Rap, 1830–1996*. New York: St. Martin's Press, 1998.

Sternheimer, Karen. *Connecting Social Problems and Popular Culture: Why Media is Not the Answer*, 2nd edition. Boulder, CO: Westview Press, 2013.

———. "Do Video Games Kill?" *Contexts* 6, no. 1 (2007), pp. 13–17.

Strinati, Dominic. *An Introduction to Theories of Popular Culture*, 2nd edition. London: Routledge, 2004.

Tilley, Carol. "Seducing the Innocent: Fredric Wertham and the Falsifications that Helped Condemn Comics." *Information & Culture: A Journal of History* 47, no. 4 (2012), pp. 383–413.

Trapunski, Edward. *Special When Lit: A Visual and Anecdotal History of Pinball*. New York: Doubleday, 1979.

Walsh, Frank. *Sin and Censorship: The Catholic Church and the Motion Picture Industry*. New Haven: Yale University Press, 1996.

Wright, Bradford W. *Comic Book Nation: The Transformation of Youth Culture in America*. Baltimore: The Johns Hopkins University Press, 2001.

Zelizer, Viviana. *Pricing the Priceless Child: The Changing Social Value of Children*. Princeton, NJ: Princeton University Press, 1985.

INDEX

Page numbers in **bold** refer to illustrations.

Abanes, Richard 143–4
Adams, Roy 80
advocacy groups 9
African Americans: changing status
  118; migration 110; and movies
  28; music 107–10; racial violence
  against 114
Agnew, Spiro T. 62
Alabama White Citizen's Council
  (AWCC) 111
alcohol abuse 29
Altschuler, Glenn C. 128
American Civil Liberties Union
  (ACLU) 140
American Library Association 143
American Psychiatric Association
  112
anti-Catholicism 37
anti-comic book crusades 73–101;
  Catholic Church 78; context 95–9;
  decline of 99–100; intellectual 75,
  77–8; and juvenile delinquency 74,
  79, 81–2, 83–4, 86–91, **89**, 96–7;
  Kefauver 85–91, **86**, **89**, 91; lessons
  100–1; New York 84–5; and

parental responsibility 83; police
  81–2; political involvement 83–91,
  86, **89**; PTAs 81, 82, 87; triggers
  78–80; United Kingdom 99;
  Wertham 91, 91–5
anti-movie crusades 23–46, 146–7;
  anti-Semitism 40; boycotts 39, 40;
  Catholic Church 37–9; Chase
  blames Jews 34–6; claims 25; The
  Code 37–9; context 42–5; decency
  czar 36; decline of 40–2; first
  censorship ordinance 23–4;
  Legion of Decency 39–40, 40;
  lessons 45–6; New York 25, 29–34,
  30; news stories 25–9, 45; and
  Sunday licensing 35
anti-music crusades 105–29; decline
  of 127–8; fears of racial integration
  107–12; jazz 107–10; and juvenile
  delinquency 107; lessons 128–9;
  politics of 124–7; PTAs 125–6;
  record burning 123; religious
  119–24; rock and roll 105–6, 109,
  110–8, **119**, 122–4; subliminal
  messages recorded backwards

124–5; the Washington Wives
125–7, 127–8
anti-pinball crusades 49–70;
appearance 50–1; and child
protection 58–61; confiscations 57;
contexts 61–6; convictions 59;
decline of 66–9; expansion 58–61;
gambling and 64–6; and juvenile
delinquency 58–61, 63–4; La
Guardia 49, 53–8, **54**, 58; lessons
69–70; and lost tax revenue 60–1;
timing 51–2
anti-Semitism 18, 34–6, 40, 111,
146–7
anti-war movement 41
arcades 19, 51, 68
Association of Comics Magazine
Publishers (ACMP) 84, 87, 90
audience segmentation 136

backwards masking 124–5
Bair, Amy Lupold 140
Balko, Radley 69
Baltimore Sun 59, 105, 108, 112
Batman and Robin 76, 91–2, 93–4
Beatlemania 120–1
Beatles, the 120–2, 124
Becker, Howard 9, 20, 135
Beckham, David 137
Ben-Yehuda, Nachman 6, 7, 14
Bernstein, Lee 61–2
Best, Joel 7–8, 15
Better Homes and Gardens 59
Billboard magazine 109
Binder, Amy 117
Birmingham, Alabama 110–2
Birnbaum, Larry 109–10
Bivins, Jason C. 120
Black, Gregory D. 39

Black, Hugo 60
Black Sabbath 124
Blackmar, Abel 32
Blondie 76
blue laws 35
Boston 58–9, 115
Bourdieu, Pierre 148
boyd, dana 141
Braceland, Francis J. 112
Breen, Joseph I. 39–40, 42, 146–7
Brooks, Darryll 117
Brown v. Board of Education 94
Buckley, Tom 67
Burnham, John C. 65

Callahans and the Murphys, The
(film) 37
Carter, Asa 110–2, 113, 136
Catechism on Motion Pictures (Chase)
34–5, 36
Catholic Church: anti-comic book
crusades 78; anti-movie crusades
37–9
Catholic World 78
censorship 145–6; comic books
81, 88; movies 23–4, 33, 36,
39, 44
Chase, William Sheafe 31, 34–6, 37,
40, 42
Chicago 60–1; censorship ordinance
23–4; comic book ban 83; pinball
ban lifted 66
Chicago Daily News 77
Chicago Daily Tribune 58, 78, 80
Chicago Tribune 26, 60–1, 68, 82, 83
child labor 43–4, 95
child pornography 138, 140
child protection 58–61
child sexual abuse 7, 67

Child Study Association of
America 87
children and childhood: changes in
meaning of 18, 43–4, 63, 95–6,
100–1, 146; criminalizing 140;
fears of corruption of 59; fears of
influence of movies on 26–8, 45;
immigrant 64; innocence 63, 80,
96; leisure time 51–2; need for
protection 44, 58–61;
vulnerability 26
Christian Broadcasting Network
(CBN) 143
Christian Science Monitor 79, 80, 81,
90, 112, 140
Chuck E. Cheese 68–9
civil rights movement 41, 114, 115
claims-makers 14
Clark, Dick 105
Cleave, Maureen 120–1
Clinton, Bill 10, 11, 14, 128
Clinton, Tennessee 111
Cohen, Stanley 6, 10, 11, 14, 59
Cold War, the 95
Cole, Nat King 111
Columbine High School massacre
1–2, 3, 6
comic books 18–9, 145; ACMP
code 84, 87, 90; banned 82, 83;
censorship 81, 88; concerns
about 74–5, 77–8; crime 76–7,
79, 82; and crime 85, 85–91, **86,
89**; crime 97–8; fears of
promotion of homosexuality
91–2, 93–4; feminized 76; genres
74; graphic images 76–7; horror
76, 87, 97–8; language use 75;
numbers 75; origins 76–7; price
74, 76; readership 73–4, 100–1;

superhero 76, 77, 77–8; and
teen pregnancy 92; threat
of 97–8; and youth violence
78–80. *see also* anti-comic book
crusades
Comic-Con 99
comics code, the 84, 87, 90
Comics Magazine Association of
America (CMAA) 90
communists and communism 40
Comstock, Anthony 74–5
Comstock Law 74–5
consumerism 43
convictions, anti-pinball crusades 59
"Cop Killer" (Ice-T) 117–8
corruption 53, 59, 62–3
Cossack v. City of Los Angeles 66
counterculture, the 67–8, 99
crack babies 15
crime: and comic books 85, 85–91,
86, 89; fascination with 61; and
movies 25–6, 26
Crime SuspenStories 88, **89**
cults 123–4
cultural change 64–5, 145
cultural hierarchies 4, 148
cultural imperialism 99

Daily Telegraph 138
Dallas Morning News 143, 144
dancing 108; interracial 110
Daniels, Les 76, 98, 99
Darien, Connecticut 58
DC Comics 76
demographics 18, 24, 25, 42–3
demonization 11–2, 118
Detroit 83, 117
deviance 12–4
Dewey, Thomas 85

Dilulio, John 15
dime novels 74–5
Dornan, Robert K. 125
drug scares 8, 15
drug use 67

economic change 42, 147
economic growth 52, 107
Edison, Thomas Alva 31
Ellington, Duke 109
Ellsworth, Robert S. 120, 122
entertainment choices, expansion
    of 146
Erikson, Kai 12
evil 33, 34, 59, 90
expert status 135–6

Facebook 136, 143
Facey, Paul W. 39
fascism 77–8
Federal Bureau of Investigation
    (FBI) 96
Fellick, Lonnie 78–9
Fine, Gary Alan 43
First Amendment rights 33, 41,
    84–5, 88, 95
first-person shooter video games 2
folk devils 11–2, 14
Ford, Henry 35–6
Forester, the Reverend Dr. J.M. 31
Fraternal Order of Police 81–2
Freed, Alan 110, 115, **119**
freedom of speech and expression 5,
    8, 98, 145–6, 147
Funk, the Reverend I. K. 25–6

Gaines, William 88, 90
gambling 50, 52, 58; addiction to 59;
    anti-pinball crusades and 64–6;
    appeal of 65; definition 50–1; La

Guardia and 53–4, 55; legalization
    65–6; mainstreaming 52; negative
    associations 65; and organized
    crime 53; proliferation of 66;
    revenues 66
gaming. *see* anti-pinball crusades
gangster films 38–9
Gans, Herbert 5
Geltman, Joani 139–40
Germany 108
Gilbert, James 63–4, 95, 97
Githens, Perry 58, 59
Goode, Erich 6, 7, 14
Gore, Al 127–8
Great Depression, the 38–9, 44, 52,
    55, 63, 76
Greenwald, Gary 122

Hajdu, David 87, 95
Harrison, George 124
Harry Potter books (Rowling) 18,
    135, 142–5
Hartford Courant 80, 82, 83, 84, 105,
    112, 113–4, 122
Hays, Will H. 36, 38
Hearst, William Randolph 76
Heins, Marjorie 64
Hendrickson, Robert 87–8, 88
high culture 4–5, 148
Hitler, Adolf 108
Hoffa, Jimmy 62
Hollings, Ernest 126
Hollywood 36, 43
homosexuality, fears of promotion
    of 91–2, 93–4
Hoover, J. Edgar 86–7

Ice-T 117–8
idleness, and immorality 52
Illinois 27

immigration 17, 18, 28, 37, 42, 45–6, 64, 145
imperialism 28
India 28
Indian casinos 66
information, control of 134
internet, the 20, 66, 69, 136
internet gambling 66
interracial violence 113–4
intimate violence 77
Irish Times 139
Italian Conference of Catholic Bishops 145

Jackson, John A. 110
Japan 106
jazz 19, 106, 107–10, 112
Jews: and the movie industry 34–6, 40, 41–2; fears of 35–6; patriotism 41–2
Jim Crow 109
John, Elton 68
Johnson, Jack 28
Jonestown tragedy, Guyana 124
Joseph Burstyn, Inc. v. Wilson 41
juvenile delinquency 18, 46; and anti-comic book crusades 74, 79, 81–2, 83–4, 86–91, **89**, 96–7; and anti-music crusades 107; and anti-pinball crusades 58–61, 63–4; arrest statistics 96–7; fear of 14–7, 97; frenzy about 73; and the movies 26–8; political response 83; rates 15, 92, 96–7, 134; statistics 96
Juvenile League, the 32

Kefauver, Estes 61–2, 74, 85–91, **86**, **89**, 91
Kennedy, Robert F. 62

Kessner, Thomas 53, 54–5
Kinsey Reports 98
Korpan, Walter 60
Ku Klux Klan 36, 109, 121

La Guardia, Fiorello 49, 53–8, **54**, 58
Lang, Howard 78–9
Larson, Bob 122, 124
Lears, Jackson 65
Led Zeppelin 124
Legion of Decency 39–40, 40
leisure time, increase in 50–1, 51–2
Lennon, John 120–1; Beatles "more popular than Jesus" 121–2
Levenson, Joseph 25
Levine, Harry 138
Lewis, Donald 125
London Evening Standard 120–1
Lopes, Paul 4, 81
Lord, Daniel A. 37
Los Angeles 66, 83
Los Angeles Sentinel 114
Los Angeles Times 26, 27, 68, 105, 122, 125
low culture 148

McCarthy-era red scare 42
McClellan, George B. Jr. 29–34, **30**, 42, 42–3, 53
McCollum, Bill 14–5
McKay, Henry D. 82
Mann Act 109
mass culture 4
Masserman, Jules 112
media attention 135–7
mediated entertainment 98–9
Menconi, Al 123, 124
micro crusades 135, 136, 142–5
Miller v. California 98
Mills, C. Wright 93

Miracle, The (film) 41
miscegenation 38, 111
moral crusaders 8–9, 9–10, 12, 16,
    19–20, 24, 34, 42, 59, 133–4, 135,
    145–8
moral decay 39
moral entrepreneurs 9, 20
moral panics 6–8, 145, 146, 146–7,
    148; activists 8–11; context 14–7;
    definition 6; focus 7; issues 7; life
    cycle 17; reach 19–20; and
    righteousness 7; snowball effect
    7–8; spread 6–7; timing 14
moral profiteers 135–7, 142
morality, guardians of 24
Motion Picture Commission 25
Motion Picture Producers and
    Distributors of America
    (MPPDA) 36
movie stars, lifestyle 36
movie theaters 23, 32–3, 43
movies: attendance 45; censorship
    23–4, 33, 36, 39, 44; The Code
    37–9; corrupting influence 18; and
    crime 25–6, 26; crusades against
    18; distribution 28; European 40;
    fears of audience vulnerability 25;
    fears of influence on children
    26–8, 45; growth of industry 23;
    independent studios 40; and moral
    decay 39; Production Code of
    America (PCA) 39–40; ratings
    system 45; regulation 45; Sunday
    licensing 35. *see also* anti-movie
    crusades
Murphy, Charles F. 90
music 19, 101; anti-authority themes
    106; audience 107; banned 108,
    110; concerns about 106–7;
considered satanic 123, 124–5, 126;
    dangers of 122; demonization 118;
    and fears of racial integration 106,
    107–12, 117, 118; heavy metal 106,
    124; idolatry 119–24; jazz 106,
    107–10, 112; performers 109;
    rap 106, 116–8; ratings system
    125–6, 127; rock and roll 101,
    105–6, 109, 110–8, **119**, 120,
    122–4, 128, 145; sales 128; and sex
    109–10; and teen pregnancy 106,
    126; and violence 105, 113–8, **119**;
    violent lyrics 117–8, 127; and youth
    culture 107; and youth violence
    106. *see also* anti-music crusades
Muslims 17
*Mutual Film Corporation v. Industrial
    Commission of Ohio* 33

Nasaw, David 44
National Association for the
    Advancement of Colored People
    (NAACP) 111
National Campaign to Prevent Teen
    and Unplanned Pregnancy 139
National Civic League 81
National Crime Victimization
    Survey 126–7
National Endowment for the Arts
    (NEA) 107
National Rifle Association (NRA) 10
Nevada, legalizes gambling 65
New York: anti-comic book crusades
    84–5; anti-movie crusades 25,
    29–34, **30**; anti-pinball crusades
    49, 53–8, **54**, 58, 59; demographic
    change 42–3; the Great
    Depression 55; jazz ban 108;
    pinball ban lifted 66–7

New York Post 2
New York Society for the
  Suppression of Vice 74–5
New York Times 2, 27, 56, 59, 66, 83,
  85, 87, 92, 93, 106, 108, 114, 118
New York Tribune 32, 32–3, 108
Newport, Rhode Island 105, 114
newspapers: anti-movie crusades
  25–9, 45; comic strips 76;
  declining circulations 142
Nietzsche, Friedrich 77
Noebel, David 120
nonconformity, expression of 16
norms, violation of 13
North, Sterling 77, 78
North Alabama White Citizen's
  Council 111

obscenity 98
Old Ironsides (film) 36
Ong, Walter 77
organized crime 51, 52–3, 55;
  focus on 61–2; and pinball 60–1,
  61–3, 69–70; Senate hearing
  broadcasts 61
outsiders: definition of 12; fear of
  20, 62
oversimplification 82

paganism 78, 144
Parent Teacher Associations 81, 82,
  87, 125–6
parenting 27–8, 83
parenting experts 139–40
Parents magazine 77
Parents Music Resource Center
  (PMRC) 126–7, 127–8
patriotism 38, 41–2
Pennsylvania 138

People's Institute, the 31–2
Pereles, Jon 118
Peters, Dan, Steve, and Jim 123
Pew Research Internet Project 141
pinball machines 18–9, 49–50, 145;
  addiction to 59; around the world
  67; banned 49, 56, 57–8, 58, 59,
  67; bans lifted 66–7; confiscation
  57; and gambling 50–1; imagery
  51; income from 56; nostalgia, for
  69; numbers 56; and organized
  crime 60–1, 61–3, 69–70; origins
  52–3; players 51, 56; potential
  threat 64; skill 56, 58; video games
  replace 68. *see also* anti-pinball
  crusades
"Pinball Wizard" (song) 68
Pittsburgh 23
Playboy 98
Poe, Edgar Allan 77
politicians: anti-comic book
  crusades 83–91, **86, 89**; anti-
  music crusades 124–7; and
  juvenile delinquency 83; and
  moral crusades 10
popular culture: audience 4, 6;
  concerns about 4–6, 7; definition
  4–5; and economic change 147;
  expansion of 5, 133–4; fears about
  18; growth of 95; increase in
  explicitness 5; pleasure of
  consumption 147–8; segmentation
  6; status 148; and technological
  change 6
Popular Science 58
poverty 16, 148
power 13–4
Presley, Elvis 110
Prevention of Cruelty to Children 31

Production Code of America (PCA)
  39–40
Prohibition 24, 29, 36–7, 52, 55,
  65, 146
*Protocols of the Wise Men of Zion,
  The* 35
psychoanalysis, popularity of 94
public attention, getting 135–7
public morality 34
Pulitzer, Joseph 76

Quigley, Martin 37

racial integration, fears of 38, 106,
  107–12, 117, 118
racism 38
rap music 106, 116–8
record burning 123
regulation 9; comic books 84, 87, 90;
  movies 37–9, 45; video games 11
Reinarman, Craig 8, 138
religious anti-music crusades 119–24
religious authority 34
religious sects 123–4
religious service attendance 122
respectability, enforcement of 5
righteousness: and moral panics 7;
  sense of 55
road rage 8
rock and roll 101, 105–6, 109, 110–8,
  119, 120, 122–4, 128, 145
Rock Around the Clock (film) 106
Roosevelt, Franklin D. 55
Roosevelt, Theodore 31
Rose, Tricia 118
Rosenberg, Ethel 94
Ross, Edward A. 27
Ross, Steven 43
Roth v. United States 98

routinization of caricature, the 138
Run-DMC 116

St. Petersburg Times 116
Salem witch trials 12
Sandy Hook Elementary School
  massecre 17
Satanism 123, 124–5, 142, 145
scapegoatism 82
Schultz, Henry E. 84, 87–8
Seduction of the Innocent (Wertham)
  91, 92–4
segregation 109–10, 110–2, 118,
  128–9, 145
Senate Subcommittee Hearings on
  Juvenile Delinquency 86–91, **89**
sex, and music 109–10
sexting 18, 20, 134, 137–42
sexuality 67
Sheehan, John 139
sin 24, 40, 69
Sklar, Robert 23
slot machines 53, 56
smartphone technology 18, 20, 128,
  134, 141. *see also* sexting
Smith, Charles Sprague 31–2
snowball effect 7
social change 24, 42
social harm 29
social media 20, 136, 143
social networking technology
  128, 135
Society for the Prevention of
  Crime 82
South Korea 67
Soviet Union 106, 108
Springhall, John 95–6
"Stairway to Heaven" (Led
  Zeppelin) 124

Star Wars figurines, burning of 123
subliminal messages 125
suicide rates 127
Sunday laws 35
superficial explanations 148
Superman 76, 77–8
Supreme Court 5, 15, 35, 84–5, 95, 98; anti-pinball crusades and 56, 57; *Joseph Burstyn, Inc. v. Wilson* 41; *Mutual Film Corporation v. Industrial Commission of Ohio* 33, 41; *Roth v. United States* 98; *United States v. Paramount Pictures, Inc.* 41
Synett, Harold C. 31

Taft, William H. 31
Tappas, Paul 82
Tarzan 76
taste communities 6
tax revenue, lost 60–1
Taylor, William Desmond 36
technological innovation 6, 134, 140
teen pregnancy 92, 106, 148; decline in 140–1; and music 126
teenagers: appearance as group 63; conceptualizing 63–4; sexual activity 140–1
television 40, 41, 94–5; ownership growth 99–100; Senate hearing on organized crime broadcasts 61
Temperance movement 24, 64
text messages: numbers sent 138. *see also* sexting
Third Reich, the 108
Thrasher, Frederic 93
threat, potential 64
Tilley, Carol L. 93–4
Tommy (The Who) 68

Toronto 67
Triangle Shirtwaist 33
Twitter 136

unemployment 16
Uniform Crime Reports (UCR) 96
United Kingdom, anti-comic book crusades 99
urbanization 18, 42, 43, 145
US Army, pinball ban 59
USA Today 139, 144

values: American 18; competing 8–9
Vatican, the 28
victimization 5
video games 7; become mainstream 17; competing values 8; concerns about 16; demonization 11–2; first-person shooter 2; growth of 2; military use 10; moral crusaders against 10; panic ebbs 17; players 5; rating system 11; replaces pinball 68; self-regulation 11; and youth violence rates 2–3, 14, 16
Vietnam War 124
violence: interracial 113–4; intimate 77; and music 105, 113–8, **119**
Volstead Act 24

Walker, Jimmy 55
Wallace, George 111
Warshow, Robert S. 93
Washington Post, The 26, 27, 93, 112, 116–7
Washington Wives, the 125–7, 127–8
Watkins, Jon 144

Wertham, Fredric 78, 91, 91–5, 135–6
white slavery 109
Who, The 68
witchcraft 142, 144
Women's National Sabbath Alliance 35
Wonder Woman 91
World War I 28, 37
World War II 40, 41–2, 52, 56–7, 110
Wright, Bradford W. 98
Wyman, Phillip 124–5

Yarroll, William H., II 125
Young, Mary de 7
young people, vulnerability 11
youth culture: and music 107; segmentation of 97
youth revolt 27
youth violence 7, 16; and comic books 74, 78–80; and music 106; and video games 2–3, 14
YouTube 136

zoot suits 105